D0325699

AGE NICOLAISEN

THE POCKET ENCYCLOPEDIA OF INDOOR PLANTS

IN COLOR

Illustrated by

PALLE BREGNHOI and OTTO FRELLO

Editor of the American Edition
JEROME EATON
Director, Old Westbury Gardens, N.Y.

MACMILLAN PUBLISHING CO., INC.
NEW YORK

First published in the English edition 1970
English text © Blandford Press Ltd,
167 High Holborn, London WC1V 6PH

World Copyright 1969
Politikens Forlag A/S
Copenhagen

All rights reserved. No part of this book
may be reproduced or transmitted in any form
or by any means, electronic or mechanical,
including photocopying, recording or by any
information storage and retrieval system,
without permission in writing from the publisher.

Library of Congress catalog number 77–91385

First American Edition 1970
Third Printing 1972
Fourth Printing 1973
Fifth Printing 1973
Sixth Printing 1974
Seventh Printing 1974
Eighth Printing 1975

THE MACMILLAN COMPANY
866 Third Avenue, New York, N.Y. 10022

Color section printed in Denmark
by F. E. Bording A/S
Text printed in England by Fletcher & Son Ltd, Norwich
and books bound by Richard Clay (The Chaucer Press), Ltd,
Bungay, Suffolk

PREFACE TO THE AMERICAN EDITION

is all too seldom that a well written European book with just the right approach to be useful, requires little adaptation for publication in the United tates.

The European household has often been considered a superior, if not the erfect environment for growing plants, and hence the popularity and great access of raising indoor plants abroad. However, it has taken Mr. Nicoisen to give us the basic facts necessary to translate these successes for the merican home. An example is the degree of healthy plant growth which is edited to the lack of wide use of central heating in many countries abroad. ctually, there are simple measures for correcting dry atmospheric conditions in American homes with central heating and these adjustments are all at are necessary to overcome such adversity. (One can, for instance, use ightly more water in caring for plants.)

In addition to showing us how to grow plants to a greater degree of erfection, the author also gets us out of our comfortable rut. Yes, when it omes to growing house plants, we are provincial. In the States it is rare to id species of plants being grown indoors beyond those one or two dozen opular varieties with which we are familiar, even though there are many hers of even greater beauty and which are equally certain to succeed. The velation of some of these exotics is all that should be necessary to arouse incurable interest.

The growing of plants is usually done by rote, from seeing our parents or ighbors performing gardening chores even before our own genuine intert has been kindled. Because of building up one's expertise in this inbred anner, it is especially valuable to get a completely independent point of ew.

It is by reading such new and clarifying thoughts as you will find in this ok that you will get the understanding necessary to cope with the many cisions that will undoubtedly arise in your pursuit of success in gardening doors.

While the physiology of plant growth is a science, it is the manner in nich the variable factors are balanced against one another that brings the ery day culture of plants into the realm of an art. The author of this book commends some techniques and materials that might be a departure from ose with which you are familiar but all of them are not only valid and oven commercially but will make your experience in growing these plants st a little more interesting.

3

Before you have gone very far in reading the plant profiles in the follow-ing chapters you probably will have made an unconscious determination as to what the author's prerequisites were in classifying any specific variety as a house plant. These include such characteristics as reasonable size and shape, outstanding color of flower or foliage, as well as its adaptation to low light intensity, dry atmospheric conditions and tolerance of less than expe... care. Naturally, the author has not included all the possible candidates but only those which, in his expert judgement, comprise the best and mo... interesting ones. However, armed with the knowledge you will ha... acquired in reading these subsequent pages, you will be able to go beyon... these varieties and make determinations of your own as to the suitability ... additional species that come to your attention and you will even be able ... decide upon the proper method for making them grow.

If I were asking the opinion and advice of a less authoritative writer, ... would be content with gently stated opinions and suggestions for pla... culture, however, I am pleased, in this instance, to have the best species ... variety *told* to me in no uncertain terms and instructions on how I *shou...* grow plants rather than how I *might* grow them. With this expert advice, ... feel that the reader is being turned in exactly the right direction and w... reach his goal via the most direct route.

JEROME A. EATON

FOREWORD

his book, which is intended first and foremost as a work of reference for ndoor gardeners', i.e. amateurs who cultivate plants indoors, in window oxes, or conservatories, lists and describes 350 different indoor plants. ne hundred and fifty of the plants dealt with are illustrated by colour ates, while a further 100 are shown in black—white—green illustrations ong with the plant descriptions. One hundred plants are not illus- ated, since they so closely resemble the others that this is not considered cessary.

The plants shown in the colour plates are numbered from 1 to 150, and c number of each is given in the plant description immediately after its ame for easy cross-reference.

In arranging the plants in sequence, the botanical system has been fol- wed closely, both in the colour plates and in the plant descriptions. Within ch family, the different species have, as far as is reasonably possible, been ted alphabetically. But in a few instances, it was more appropriate to give description of the most popular subject, the growth and culture of which is such importance that it has been printed outside the alphabetical quence.

The book is prefaced by a short introduction concerning indoor plants, eir use and care, along with some indications of the culture requirements the plants. This is followed by the colour plates and the plant descrip- ons, set out on an identical basic pattern which includes the name of the mily and species, habitat, growth, use, culture requirements and other tails of care, pests and diseases, so that the reader may easily find the formation he requires, whether he wishes to identify an unknown plant or tain information on use and care. The book's function as a work of ference is augmented by a comprehensive index.

With regard to the indication of names, the family name is given in its ficial Latin form, while the names of the genus and species are both given Latin and English wherever possible. In the English edition, the R.H.S. *ctionary of Gardening* has been consulted.

The plants were selected and the text prepared by Cand. Hort. Åge colaisen, a municipal gardener, while the illustrations are the work artists Palle Bregnhøi and Otto Frello. Both the illustrations and the mes of the plants have been checked by botanical gardeners at the penhagen University botanical gardens, Cand. Hort. Ernst Floto and ndrology Professor at the Royal College of Agriculture and Veterinary

Science in Copenhagen, Dr. Phil. Johan Lange, to whom the editor is mo
indebted.

The book may be used internationally, and will be published in Britai
France, Holland, Italy, Norway, Spain, Sweden, Germany and the Unit
States.

THE EDITOR

INTRODUCTION

The term covers all foliage and flowering plants which can be cultivated indoors on window-sills, in special flower windows or bay windows, in halls, in staircases, on verandas, or in patios and conservatories.

All types of plants can be used as indoor plants: trees and bushes, shrubs, bulbous and tuberous plants and annuals. This great variety means that use and care are subject to all kinds of different requirements. Some indoor plants can be kept indoors for many years in the same situation; other types are seasonal and must be discarded after flowering. The same plant may behave differently in different climatic conditions. One plant may, for example, be tree-like in tropical regions, where there is no great fluctuation in climate, whereas it may be cultivated or may thrive as a sub-shrub in temperate regions—in colder climates even as an annual.

This irregularity may also be encountered where the plant is cultivated indoors in an artificial climate. The intensity of the light and relative degree of air humidity, in particular, may vary here so greatly that certain plants appear under some conditions to be tree-like perennials, while under different conditions they may be short-lived herbaceous plants. The reason why certain indoor plants often fare badly is not therefore necessarily lack of skill on the part of the gardener but rather the wrong climate in the room or winter garden.

CHOICE OF INDOOR PLANTS

An 'indoor gardener' naturally wants his plants to grow as well as possible, and beginners must therefore start with the 'easy' varieties. The more experienced, on the other hand, may like to try their skill with plants whose culture and care impose particularly exacting demands, and the choice of plants in this book takes both groups into account. The plant descriptions make it clear whether the plant is an 'easy' or 'difficult' one, and warnings are given against trying out certain varieties which do not normally thrive under indoor cultivation. Enthusiasts are encouraged to try out new plants and to specialise in types which present a particular challenge to their skills. There are indoor gardeners who have concentrated on orchids, and others who have specialised in ferns, plants of the pineapple family (bromeliads) or cacti. There are infinite possibilities which this book may perhaps stimulate the reader to try.

Thousands of plants can be cultivated in an artificial indoor climate, but the selection presented here only covers those which are generally cultivated or may reasonably be expected to be obtainable from nurserymen. Many of the plants dealt with are not grown in the large nurseries, but must be looked for among the small commercial gardeners who grow a large and varied range. It may be that some can only be bought as seeds from home or foreign seed merchants, or may have to be obtained from botanical gardens

In the plant descriptions the country or place of origin is given, often with a short description of the local geographic or climatic conditions, which may provide the reader with a picture of the cultural requirements or possibilities for use indoors. The appearance of the plants is only briefly indicated, and the text must therefore be read in conjunction with the colour plates or the illustrations appearing with the plant descriptions. The most important characteristics, however, as for example growth form, leaves, flowers, fragrance if any, fruit and height of indoor culture, are included.

An indication is also given as to whether the indoor plant is particularly suitable for cultivation in an ordinary window-box, in a conservatory or under extreme conditions, such as deep shade or burning sun. Possibilities for growth out of doors during the summer as a balcony or tub plant are also mentioned. Information is given as to whether the plant is a perennial indoor variety or a seasonal type which must be discarded after flowering.

Within each species there are often quite a few different varieties which may make for a pleasant change in the window-box. In such cases the most important varieties are mentioned, with an indication of varying flower or leaf colours or other special characteristics.

The Englerian system has been followed closely in the order in which the plants have been arranged, both in the colour plates and in the plant descriptions. Botanical research, however, is constantly bringing about changes in the sequence applied in the system, and a book such as this can therefore only remain in conformity with the correct official system for a short time. Since, for technical reasons, the illustrations and descriptions cannot be relocated in each new edition, we have decided to follow a single slightly older system, specially adapted to the indoor gardener's requirements, but which does not incorporate the most recent decisions of the International Botanical Congress.

THE CULTURE REQUIREMENTS OF INDOOR PLANTS

Indoor plants impose a wide variety of demands on soil, fertiliser, water, light, heat and air, which are all detailed under the appropriate headings in the individual plant descriptions.

In an ordinary room it will usually only be possible to satisfy these demands approximately. Homes are primarily intended to meet the needs and wishes of those who live in them rather than the requirements of plants which may be kept there, so it is not surprising that an indoor atmosphere often does not suit the plant at all well. The size of the window may limit the intensity of the light, and central heating makes for high temperatures and

r which is too dry, an atmosphere in which some plants fare particularly
.dly.

The combination of climatic factors is possibly even more important than
e individual factors alone. It may thus be of little use to have the right
mperature if there is not the corresponding optimum amount of light and
r humidity in the room. Cacti, for example, thrive outstandingly well in
y, centrally heated air, but the amount of light in rooms is much too small
.ring most months of the year.

By changing the temperature and air humidity, by ensuring the right
gree of soil moisture, by adding artificial light and by applying the correct
sage of nutrition to the pot soil, one can get very close to the optimum
nditions for some indoor plants, but these conditions may not suit the
her plants which are being cultivated in the room. The room atmosphere
ust therefore remain a compromise which takes account first and foremost
the people who live there, and then of the plants.

il

e pot soil must be thoroughly porous, so that air and moisture can easily
netrate. An artificially blended soilless mixture can be bought which
nsists of peat with the most important nutrient materials added. This suits
any plant types, but where experience has shown that plants fare badly in
ch a mixture, this is expressly indicated in the descriptions. Otherwise, the
thusiast may make an excellent potting soil for himself by mixing a good,
ht loam with peat, well-rotted manure and fine grit or sharp sand.

Plants which make special demands on the composition of the soil are
ost often those with a poorly developed root system, or with roots which
rive best under particular chemical conditions, for example acid soil with
ow reaction rate (denoted by pH), or in an especially alkaline soil with a
gh reaction rate. Neutral soil has a rate of pH 7, acid soil down to pH 3
d alkaline soil up to pH 8.

The reaction rate of a soil blend can be raised by the addition of calcium
simply by watering with ordinary tap water, which usually has a high
lcium content, and can be lowered by the addition of 'acid' nutrients, such
potassium sulphate. Most indoor plants like a soil mixture with a reaction
te which is not too alkaline; therefore, on daily watering, 1 gram of
mmonium sulphate per litre ($\frac{1}{4}$ oz. per gallon) should be added to keep the
action rate suitably low.

Mixing in sand makes the soil lighter, but at the same time it will then dry
t more quickly, so it must be watered frequently. The addition of peat
ings about an increased capacity for the absorption of moisture, so a soil
this type does not need such frequent watering. The porosity of the soil
n be increased, without altering its chemical composition, by adding such
aterials as 'Styromuld', 'Perlite' or 'Vermiculite'.

If ordinary clay flower-pots are used, a considerable amount of evapora-
n from the surface of the pot must be expected, whereas plastic pots allow

9

only a small amount of evaporation or none at all. Plants requiring consta
moisture at their roots thus do especially well in plastic pots.

Feeding

The soil content of a flower-pot is very small and, depending on the appeti
of the plant in question, the nutrient materials it contains are used up after
certain period of time. Therefore care should be taken to feed the plants
the appropriate intervals. Some plants should be given small quantities
nourishment at short but regular intervals; other, more demanding varieti
must be given larger amounts at longer intervals. One or two plants hard
need to be fed at all, but prefer their soil to be changed completely eve
year or six months. Nourishment in powder form should *never* be given wi
dry pot soil, so make sure that the soil is thoroughly moist beforehar
otherwise there is a danger that the artificial fertiliser may scorch the roo
It is easier to apply a liquid fertiliser, which is added to the water and can
used on dry soil.

Any one of the mixed fertilisers available from dealers may be used f
nourishment. These have closely controlled contents of the three ma
nutrient materials, nitrogen, potassium and phosphorus, and also conta
small amounts of the necessary trace elements such as manganese, ma
nesium, iron, boron and many others.

It is just as easy—and considerably cheaper—to make your ov
fertiliser mixture. This may consist of 100 grams (3 oz.) of potassiu
nitrate, 100 grams (3 oz.) of calcium phosphate and 200 grams (6 oz.)
ammonium sulphate. All three chemicals can be purchased from a chem
and mixed together, but they must be kept dry, otherwise the mixtu
becomes lumpy. The powder dissolves easily in water, and with ea
application 1–3 grams per litre ($\frac{1}{4}$–1 oz. per gallon) should be used,
specified in the individual plant descriptions.

Do not use too much fertiliser, as this will scorch the roots. On the oth
hand, if too little is used, there is the danger that the plant will be stunted
its growth. Never feed young seedlings, newly re-potted plants or diseas
plants, and never administer nourishment during the darkest period of t
winter, when the plant is not able to use and convert the salts in the fertilise

Some plants need special treatment with acid nutrition, and this
indicated in the descriptions dealing with these particular types.

In order to give particularly vigorous plants a good start, what is kno
as a *basic nutrient* may be given, which consists of mixing a long-acti
fertiliser in with the pot soil itself before planting. For this, you can use a
good, natural organic fertiliser.

Water

A large percentage of every plant consists of water, which is a vital requi
ment since plants absorb all forms of nourishment dissolved in water, a
can only breathe and assimilate in a certain level of air humidity.

In nature, water penetrates through the surface of the soil and down to the plant's roots where it is absorbed. The best method of watering is therefore in most cases to administer the water from above on to the soil ball. Some plants will not tolerate water in the soil, and it is best to water them through base dishes. Any water which the plant has not been able to absorb in the space of half an hour must be poured away. Many species of the pineapple family have very weakly developed roots, and it is best to water them through the central growth.

Tap water often contains calcium or disinfectants, such as chlorine, which plants as a rule do not like. Calcium in the water changes the acid level in the soil, and ugly spots may be produced on leaves and stems; rainwater—or some other calcium free water—should therefore be used, and indeed this is essential in the case of some plants such as azaleas, camellias or gardenias.

Water must always have the chill taken off it, since the use of ice-cold tap water can give plants a 'cold shock'. Most plants should always be given water at room temperature, up to minimum 16° C. (65° F.).

Many plants have a rhythmic life cycle, alternating between periods of growth and rest. Resting periods tend to coincide either with the winter or with the dry season of the plant's native habitat, and if the resting period corresponds to our own winter the plants may be less suitable for us, since we prefer indoor plants which flower and grow green at that time. This only applies to herbaceous or deciduous plants. However, the selection of plants in this book covers a range of varieties with a life cycle of this kind, which are such splendid plants indoors and in conservatories, as well as on terraces and in window-boxes, that we would not wish to leave them out and, for practical reasons, must include them in the indoor plants category.

The following might be a basic rule for watering: Give plenty of water each time, and let the pot soil dry out almost completely between each watering. Watering in dribbles is as bad as no watering at all.

Light

All green plants require light in order to be able to grow and develop. Sunlight may be replaced by artificial light, but for ordinary conditions this need not be taken into consideration.

A plant's need for a large amount of light does not always coincide with its capacity to tolerate direct sunlight. Diffused light, i.e. without direct sunshine, provides even and agreeable lighting for many plants. A large window facing north, provided there are no buildings casting a shadow or shrubbery outside, is an excellent growth spot for many plants. But, generally speaking, north-facing windows tend to look out on to neighbouring houses or dense shrubbery, and for that reason only plants which are amenable to shade are likely to thrive in these locations.

Windows facing east or west usually offer the best possibilities for the cultivation of indoor plants. In windows facing south, only plants which

require both a high light intensity and high daytime temperatures are likel
to do well. It is often an advantage to shade the flower-pot against dire
sunlight, so that the pot soil does not heat up too much thereby scorchin
the plant's roots.

Where plants have a pronounced dependence on the length of the day,
is possible to vary this artificially by creating darkness during light perioc
and providing additional light during dark periods, thus influencing th
flowering pattern. Some in this category we call short-day plants—thos
which flower when the day is less than twelve hours long—and others long
day plants—those which produce buds when night is shorter than day.

Heat

The vast majority of indoor plants need a temperature of over $0°$ C. ($32°$ F
and die when exposed to frost. Some, especially tropical varieties, are s
sensitive that they suffer slight damage at temperatures below minimur
$10°$ C. ($50°$ F.). On the other hand, they can withstand quite high tempera
tures, as long as the level of air humidity and the right amount of wate
enables them to do so.

During the resting periods most plants require lower temperatures tha
during their growth period. Even 'all-year-round' plants have a certai
rhythm, and prefer lower temperatures during the dark season. This may t
difficult to provide for in living-rooms with central heating; we, after al
prefer higher room temperatures during the winter. The ideal indoor plan
are therefore those which thrive best in living areas with unnatural climat
conditions during the winter.

No indoor plant thrives next to a stove or above a coal fire, and only ver
few grow well above a radiator.

Air

The reason for the recent fashion for house plants is to be sought in ou
changed patterns of living. In former times in old houses the doors ar
windows were so poorly sealed that damp air from outside penetrated
against the heated room air, and if there is a growth factor of speci
importance to plants it is the degree of humidity in the air.

The air in centrally heated rooms is very dry, and must be made mor
humid by sprinkling the plant with lukewarm water, using either an aerose
or a syringe. Weekly sponging of the leaves removes dust and gives them
better chance of functioning; during the summer this is best achieved t
leaving the plants to stand outside on a rainy day.

Very few plants will tolerate draughts, and should therefore not be place
near doors and windows which are often opened.

OTHER FORMS OF CARE REQUIRED

Besides trying to satisfy the various culture requirements of indoor plants
best one can, daily care also involves a number of indoor gardeners' chor

hich are of additional importance to their well-being. These include re-
potting, pruning, supporting, propagation and protection against pests and
seases.

aily care

While attending daily to the plants—giving water and any nourishment
quired and providing supports where necessary—it is also important to
remove withered leaves, flowers and shoots if these are seen.

At intervals one should also break up the surface soil in the pot, so that it
remains porous and easy for water to penetrate. Many indoor plants,
however, have roots which are so close to the surface that they would be
stroyed by this procedure. Instead it is possible to 'top-dress' these
varieties, i.e. cover the pot soil with a very thin layer of loamless compost,
peat or something similar.

-potting

gorous indoor plants use up the nutrients in the soil relatively fast. Even
here this nourishment is supplemented by added fertiliser, the roots must
om time to time have fresh soil. On the one hand, chemicals may become
ecipitated in the soil, so that the roots are scorched, and on the other
nd, the physical structure of the soil changes, so that the roots have
ficulty in forcing their way through and water and air cannot easily
penetrate.

It is best to re-pot simultaneously with the start of the new growth in the
rly spring. Old, thickened roots should be removed carefully, and new
sic fertiliser mixed into the fresh pot soil. At the same time, arrange for
od drainage by laying crocks (i.e. broken pieces of flower-pot, crockery,
.), sand or gravel in the bottom of the pot.

Water generously immediately after re-potting, but do not water too
ely during the period which follows, until the new roots have developed.
oid feeding altogether during the first two months after re-potting.

uning

ants which have a tree-like growth must be pruned from time to time,
rtly so as to contain them in a restrained situation such as a confined
ndow space and partly in order to promote better flowering or vegetative
velopment. Pruning may be undertaken simultaneously with re-potting,
t otherwise the best time is in the spring before new growth begins.
uning may often provide material for propagation in the form of woody
herbaceous cuttings.

Stopping of herbaceous top shoots by means of pinching out the top-most
oots during the growth period promotes a better development of lateral
anches, and in many cases also more luxuriant flowering.

Disbudding, which is for example used for chrysanthemums and roses involves the removal of side buds beneath a terminal bud so that the latt may grow particularly vigorously and give larger, better formed flowers.

Supports

Most indoor plants can do without supports. Large ornamental varieti such as Ficus, on the other hand, frequently need some kind of suppo especially when they are kept in darker positions where the growth w automatically strive towards the light. The best support to use is a bamb stick to which the plant is tied with raffia, string or 'Twist-it', thin steel wi wound with green paper.

Trellis plants, i.e. twining or climbing varieties, require some form trellis upon which they can fasten. Some of them are equipped with tendr or aerial roots; others cling by the stalks or leaf stems twining themselv around the trellis, which may consist of vertical and horizontal bamb canes, trellis work made of steel wire, or a network made of fine-mesh fi netting.

Always take care that the string and trellis do not cut into parts of t plant.

PROPAGATION

A number of indoor plants can be propagated by simple division when potting, others by cuttings of side or top shoots, rooted into soil mixed wi sand, for which a propagating unit is very suitable, with well sealed, hum air which will assist the developments of roots. By placing the plant-box flower-pot containing the cuttings over 'bottom heat', for example above radiator, more rapid root formation and development of the new plant ensured. The use of root stimulating agents such as 'Seradix', 'Rootone' 'Hormodin' greatly assists root formation in varieties which are otherw difficult to propagate from cuttings in plant windows.

Finally, a number of indoor plants can be propagated by planting see many of these can be bought from seed merchants and sown in flower-p on window-sills in the spring.

PROTECTION AGAINST PESTS AND DISEASE

The most common pests are greenfly, mealy bugs, nematodes, scale insec snails and slugs, red spider mites, springtails, thrips, wood lice and earwi These can be combated by spraying or dusting with 'Lindane' or the l toxic 'Malathion', which, however, must be used with care because of th poisonous effects. When giving this treatment, take the plants into a cell conservatory, or outdoors in mild weather; never treat them in the hou itself. Minor attacks can be stopped before they have a drastic effect, severely affected plants must be thrown out.

The most common diseases are grey mould, mildew, root rot and st canker. These fungus diseases can be combated by spraying, dusting

atering with 'Thiram' or 'Captan': always follow carefully the instructions
r use printed on the package.

The failure of indoor plants to grow satisfactorily, however, often stems
om disrupting factors other than those caused by pests or fungus diseases.
amage from cold or frost, lack of light or damage from excess light, too
uch watering, use of water containing calcium, drought, scorching of roots
sulting from incorrect feeding, top scorching and re-potting at the wrong
ne are the most common reasons why indoor plants fail to do well or take
a sickly appearance. Indoor gardeners must therefore concentrate in the
st place on correct day-to-day care in order to obtain good results.

IE POSITION OF INDOOR PLANTS IN THE HOUSE

'hile the living-rooms in the newer houses often have built-in flower-
oughs, there are few possibilities in an older house, with ordinary sills at
ch window, to grow a varied selection of indoor plants. These are kept in
eir pots in rows, the pots perhaps having special outer containers made of
orcelain, ceramic material or copper. Plants must never be placed directly
these containers, however.

Special flower windows can be arranged by planting indoor plants in a
atertight trough or container of soil, which is then placed on the window-
l, on the floor in front of the window or on a flower display table. Care
ust be taken to ensure that the container is sufficiently deep, since larger
ants require at least 30 cm. (1 ft.) of soil. Flat boxes or dishes are
isuitable for planting, if the plants are to remain in them for extended
riods without re-potting.

The ideal position for indoor plants is in a flower window, with glass
tween both the outside and the inside of the room. Between these two
ndows an artificial climate can be created with a suitably high tempera-
re and degree of air humidity, which may suit many plants particularly
ell, especially the tropical and sub-tropical types. With the aid of a
ermometer and humidity gauges, the atmosphere can be kept under con-
ol and regulated to the appropriate levels. In flower windows, the daylight
n be supplemented during the dark season by artificial light from an
ectric light bulb or a fluorescent tube; this will promote growth and
dding, and many plants will more easily overcome the inhibiting effects of
nter darkness in this way. The climate in a flower window can be con-
olled using thermostats and other mechanical aids, and natural growth
nditions reproduced for primeval forest plants, desert plants and others
quiring special environments.

The flower window must be treated as a whole, so that the individual
ants set each other off. It is an advantage not to select too many special
es, but to keep to plants which belong to the same botanical or ecological
oup (plant community), because within these groups there are always
rieties which also belong together aesthetically. Perhaps it is well to warn
loor gardeners against the procedure adopted by some flower decoration

specialists in planting out so-called mixed flower arrangements, whe special emphasis is placed on the contrast produced by the different le shapes and colours, flower shades or growth forms. A cheerful, gree background for the general furnishing plan of the room is more important the choice of indoor plants than a dramatic effect of colours and shapes.

Indoor plants can contribute to an improvement in the indoor atm sphere to the benefit of those who live in the house. The plants will, by t nature of their growth, increase the oxygen content of the air and raise t degree of air humidity, so that the air inside the house becomes mo comfortable to live in; this is of special significance in modern, we insulated houses, where the renewal of the air is made more difficult by t use of modern building techniques.

1   **1. Cyrtomium falcatum**

2. Platycerium bifurcatum
Stag-horn Fern
a. Plant attached to an old log

3. Auracaria excelsa
Norfolk Island Pine

3

4

5

Cyperus alternifolius
Umbrella Plant

Oplismenus imbecilis
"Variegatus"

6. **Howea belmoreana**
Kentia Palm

7. Aglaonema pseudobracteatum
a. Leaf of *A. roebellinii,*
b. Leaf of *A. oblongifolium curtisii*

7 a   7   7 b

8

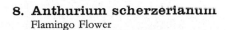

8. Anthurium scherzerianum
Flamingo Flower

9. Anthurium crystallinum

9

10. **Dieffenbachia picta**
Dumb Cane
a. Plant 1/20th scale
11. **Dieffenbachia leopoldii**

11

10

10 a

12. Monstera pertusa
a. Plant 1/15th scale

12

13

13. Spathiphyllum patinii
White Sails

14. Zantedeschia aethiopica
Arum Lily

14

15

15. Rhoeo discolor

16. Tradescantia albiflora
Wandering Jew
a. Plant 1/20th scale

17. Zebrina pendula
a. Plant 1/20th scale

16

17

17 a

18

18. Agapanthus orientalis
African Lily

19 b

19. Aloe variegata
Partridge-breasted Aloe
a. Flowering plant
b. Single non-flowering plant

19 a

20

20. Chlorophytum comosum variegatum
Spider Plant

21. Dracaena deremensis

22. Dracena marginata

23. **Hyacinthus orientalis**
Hyacinth
a. "Anne Marie"
b. "Yellow Hammer"
c. "L'Innocence"
d. Bulb
e-g. Three stages of cultivation in gla

24. Lilium auratum
a. Plant 1/15th scale

24 a

24

25 a

25

25. **Sanseveria trifasciata**
Mother-in-Law's Tongue
a. *Laurentii* variety

26. **Tulipa gesneriana**
a. "Brilliant Star"
b. "Bellona"
c. Bulb

27. **Tulipa praestans "Fusilier"**

28

3. Aechmea fasciata
4. Billbergia windii

29

30

30a

30. **Nidularium innocentii**
    a. Plant 1/10th scale

31. **Tillandsia cyanea**

32. **Vriesia splendens**

31

32

33. Agave americana
Century Plant

34. Clivia miniata
Kaffir Lily

35. Haemanthus puniceus
a. Showing flower bud

36. Hippeastrum hortorum
Amaryllis
a. Bulb

35 a

35

36

36 a

37. Narcissus pseudonarcissus
Daffodil
a. Bulb

38. Narcissus poetaz "Geranium"

37 a

37

38

39. Sprekelia formosissima
Jacobean Lily

39

40 a

40

40. Vallota speciosa
Scarborough Lily
a. Plant 1/19th scale

41. Cattleya labiata
Cattleya
a. Mauve variety
b. Flower of white variety

43. Paphiopedilum hybridum
Slipper Orchid

44 a

44

44. Odontoglossum grande
a. Flowers life size

45. Oncidium ornithorhynchum
a. Flowers life size

45 a

45

46. Maranta leuconeura kerchoveana
Prayer Plant
a. Flower life size

46 a

47

47. Ficus benjamina
a. Plant 1/20th scale

48. Ficus carica
Fig

49. Ficus elastica
India Rubber Plant

49

50. Ficus pumila
Creeping Fig

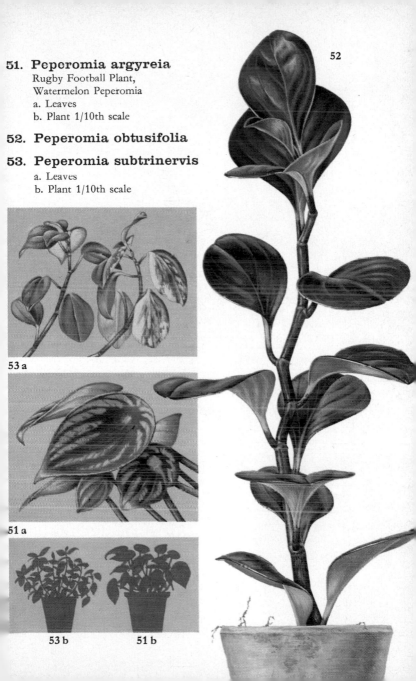

51. Peperomia argyreia
Rugby Football Plant,
Watermelon Peperomia
a. Leaves
b. Plant 1/10th scale

52. Peperomia obtusifolia

53. Peperomia subtrinervis
a. Leaves
b. Plant 1/10th scale

52

53 a

51 a

53 b   51 b

54. Dianthus caryophyllus
Carnation

55. Bougainvillea glabra
a. Plant 1/20th scale

55

55 a

56. Argyroderma testiculare
57. Conophytum springbokensis
58. Faucaria tigrina
59. Fenestraria rhopalophylla

62

60. **Lithops pseudotruncatella**
61. **Pleiospilos bolusii**
62. **Echinocactus grusonii**
   Mother-in-law's Chair

63. **Mamillaria hidalgensis**

64. **Opuntia phaecantha** (form)
Prickly Pear

65. **Selenicereus grandiflorus**
Night-flowering Cereus

64   63

66

66. Rhipsalidopsis rosea
67. Schlumbergera bridgesii
Christmas Cactus

68. Epiphyllum hybridum
  a. White variety
  b. Flower of red variety

69. Passiflora coerulea
  Passion Flower

68 a

68 b

70 b

70 a

70. Begonia cheimantha
"Gloire de Lorraine"
(B. socotrana X B. dregei)
a. Red variety
b. Flower of white variety

71. Begonia rex-cultorum

71

72 b

72 c

72 d

72 a

73

Begonia tuberhybrida
a. White variety
b-d. Flowers of other varieties

Camellia japonica

74. Pelargonium x domesticum
Regal Pelargonium
(U.S.A. Martha Washington Geranium)

75. Pelargonium x hortorum
Geranium

76. Pelargonium peltatum
Ivy-leaved Geranium

77. Impatiens walleriana
Busy Lizzie

78. Fortunella japonica
Kumquat

78

79

79. Sparmannia africana
African Hemp

80

80. Abutilon megatopamicum
Brazilian Abutilon

**81. Abutilon striatum
thompsonii**
Thompson's Abutilon

81

82. Hibiscus rosa-sinensis
Hibiscus
a. Double-red form
b. Flower of yellow variety

82 b   82 a

83 a

83

83. **Codiaeum variegatum**
Croton
a. Plant 1/20th scale

84. **Euphorbia pulcherrima**
Poinsettia
a. Red variety
b. Pink variety
c. White variety

84 b

84 a

84 c

85

85 a

86

86 a

85. Euphorbia milii
Crown of Thorns
a. Plant 1/10th scale

86. Euphorbia pugniformis
a. Plant 1/10th scale

87a

87b

87

88

Bryophyllum daigremontianum
a-b. Young plantlets

Bryophyllum tubiflorum

Crassula portulacea
Jade Plant

89

93

90. Crassula falcata
91. Echeveria gibbiflora metalli

92. Echeveria elegans
93. Kalanchoe blossfeldiana

92

91

94

96. Rosa hybrida
a. Plant 1/20th scale

96

96 a

97. Cytisus canariensis
Genista
a. Plant 1/10th scale

97

97 a

98. Acacia cyanophylla
a. Plant 1/20th scale

99. Acacia dealbata decurrens
Mimosa

99   98 a   98

100. Fuchsia hybrida

a. Flower with red sepals
   and violet corolla
b. Flower of *F. fulgens* hybrid
c. Flower with red sepals
   and white corolla

101. Punica granatum

Pomegranate
a-b. Flowers and bud, life size

101

101 b   **101**

102. Eucalyptus globulus
Blue Gum
a. Plant 1/10th scale

102 a   102

105

103

105

105 a

104

106. Erica gracilis
Christmas Heather
a. Sprig shown life size

107. Rhododendron simsii
Indian Azalea
a. Pink
b. Red
c. White

106 a

107 a

107 b

107 c

$(NH_4)_2 SO_4$

108. Cyclamen persicum giganteum
Cyclamen
a. Pink
b. Red flower
c. White flower

109. Primula malacoides
Fairy Primrose
a. Flower, life size

110. Primula kewensis

108 c

108 b

108 a

110

109 a

09

113. Pharbitis tricolor
Morning Glory

113

114

114. Brunfelsia calycina
a. Plant 1/10th scale

114 a

115. Cestrum purpureum
a. Plant 1/10th scale

115

115 a

116. Datura suaveolens
Angel's Trumpet
a. Plant 1/10th scale

116

116 a

117. **Solanum capsicastrum**
Christmas Cherry

118. **Calceolaria herbeohybrida**
Slipper Flower

119

119. Achimenes longiflora

120. Hypocyrta radicans
Clog plant

121 a

121

121. Columnea hybrida
a. Plant 1/10th scale

122. Saintpaulia ionantha
African Violet
a. Pink variety

122

122 a

123. Sinningia speciosa
Gloxinia

125. **Aphelandra squarrosa**
Zebra Plant, Tiger Plant

126. **Beloperone guttata**
Shrimp Plant

127. Fittonia argyroneura
a. Plant 1/5th scale

127

127 a

128. Thunbergia alata
Black-eyed Susan

129

129 a

129. Coleus blumei
Coleus
a. Spray of "Bienvenu"

130. Plectranthus australis
a. Plant 1/15th scale

130

130 a

131. Clerodendrum speciosissimum
a. Plant 1/15th scale

131 a

131

132 a

132 b

132. Lantana camara
a. Spray of white-flowered variety
b. Plant 1/10th scale

132

133. Jasminum polyanthum
Jasmine
a. Plant 1/10th scale

134. Allamanda neriifolia
a. Plant 1/10th scale

133

133 a

134 a   134

135. Dipladenia sanderii
a. Plant 1/10th scale

136. Nerium oleander
Oleander
a. Plant 1/20th scale
b. Leaf of variegated form

135 a

135

136 b

136 a   136

137

137. Hoya bella
138. Hoya carnosa
Wax Flower

139 a

139

139. Stephanotis floribunda
Bridal Flower
a. Plant 1/20th scale

**140. Bouvardia longifolia
humboldtii**

141

141. Coffea arabica
Coffee
a. Part of plant 1/20th scale

141 a

142

142. Gardenia jasminoides
Gardenia
a. Part of plant 1/15th scale

142 a

143. Ixora coccinea
Ixora

144. Manettia inflata
a. Plant 1/10th scale

111a

144

145. Viburnum tinu
Laurustinus

146. Campanula isophylla alba
Bellflower

147. Campanula isophylla
a. Plant 1/10th scale

147 a

148 b   148 d   148 c

148. Chrysanthemum morifolium hortorum
Chrysanthemum
a. Yellow variety
b. Single white
c. Single bronze
d. Incurved mauve

149. Gazania splendens

150. Senecio cruentus
Cineraria
a. Red variety
b. Blue variety

150 b

150 a

PLANT DESCRIPTIONS AND CULTIVATION

sic Liquid Fertiliser

recommended by the author:

3 oz. (100 grams) potassium nitrate
3 oz. (100 grams) calcium phosphate
6 oz. (200 grams) ammonium sul-
ate

Mix together but keep dry for storage
til it is to be used. The powder will
solve easily in water, and with each
plication from $\frac{1}{8}$ to $\frac{1}{2}$ oz. per gallon
3 grams per litre) should be used, as
cified in the individual plant descrip-
ns. This is the fertiliser used through-
the book.

f a proprietary liquid fertiliser is
d instead, follow the directions given
n it.

laginellaceae

aginella martensii

bitat: Hot humid valleys in Mexico.
wth: Dense fronds with filigree-like
les in delicate light green shades.
ght: 25 cm. (10 in.).
: Best in a window facing north or as
and cover in conservatories.
: Light soil, rich in humus, e.g. leaf
ld.
ding: Weak basic liquid fertiliser, 2
as per litre ($\frac{1}{2}$ oz. per gallon) every 2

Adiantum cuneatum

weeks (April–October). The roots may
be sensitive to excessive artificial fertiliser.
Water: Give plenty of water, and never
allow to dry out.
Light: Shade or half-shade, never direct
sunlight.
Heat: Summer—fresh, warm air
without any draught. Winter at least
15° C. (60° F.). Rest period October–
February.
Syringing: On hot days, but not during
the winter.
Re-potting: March, in flat bowls or pans.
Propagation: Divide or layer rooting of
shoots in the spring.

Polypodiaceae

Adiantum cuneatum

Maidenhair Fern

Habitat: Tropical rain forests in South
America.
Growth: Light and elegant, dark shoots
with finely divided light leaves. The
leaves have dark sporangia on their
undersides.
Use: In warm rooms the ferns are excellent indoor plants. They may be kept in
the shade or half-shade all the year, but
never put them in the direct sunlight.

Selaginella martensii

Cut stems may be used as green backing for mixed bouquets.

Soil: Humus-rich soil with high peat content. Soilless mixture may be used. The reaction should be slightly acid.

Feeding: Very weak doses of basic liquid fertiliser. Sensitive to nutrient salts, hence only 1 gram per litre ($\frac{1}{4}$ oz. per gallon) per week (March–August).

Water: Plenty of water during the summer growth period, sensitive to drought. Winter, moderate watering. Do not wet the leaves of young plants, but water around the outer edge of the pot or into the base dish.

Light: Best in windows facing north or at a distance from the window. Good decoration in halls, corridors, etc., where there is little daylight.

Heat: Summer, normal temperature; winter, 12–16° C. (55–60° F.).

Air: Moist air March–August during development of new shoots. Dry winter air does no harm.

Re-potting: Early spring.

Propagation: Natural propagation takes place with the aid of minute, almost microscopic, spores which may be sown on damp peat, but this method takes a long time. Division of larger plants best in March.

Asplenium nidus

Asplenium bulbiferum

Habitat: Tropical rain forests.

Growth: Pale, feathery foliage. Along the strongest leaf veins, miniature plants develop on the surfaces of the leaves; these may be detached and planted up in small pots.

Use: Best in special flower windows or warm conservatories. Less suitable as an indoor plant.

Cultivation: As for *Adiantum cuneatum* but requires somewhat higher temperature. Summer, as warm as possible; winter, not below minimum 12° C. (54° F.).

Other species: See below.

Asplenium nidus

Bird's Nest Fern

Growth: Tropical epiphyte (a plant which grows on another). Large leaves undivided around the edges, like a miniature banana leaf. These leaves spring from a rosette, the centre of which is rather like a bird's nest.

Use and culture: As for *Asplenium bulbiferum*.

Cyrtomium falcatum

Habitat: Eastern Asia.

Growth: Young shoots rolled up like bishops' croziers; older leaves shiny and leathery (coriaceous). leaves have dense sporangia on undersides.

Asplenium bulbiferum

se: Good indoor plant in shady situa-
...on.

...lture: As for *Adiantum cuneatum*,
...t will stand somewhat lower tempera-
...res.

...ephrolepsis exaltata

...bitat: Tropical America.

...owth: Metre-long, feathery leaves
...diating outwards from the central
...owing point. These leaves may take
...ot at their tips and form new plants,
...e runners from a strawberry plant.

...e: A good indoor plant in a warm
...om. The most rewarding of the indoor
...ns.

...lture: High room temperature; win-
... not below minimum 12° C. (55° F.).
...mid air, but no draught or direct sun-
...t.

...pagation: By runners which will take
...t.

...rieties 'Rooseveltii' with single fea-
...r-pattern leaves, and 'Whitmannii'
...n double feather-pattern leaves.

...tycerium bifurcatum   (2)

...g-horn Fern

...bitat: Tropical areas in Africa,
...stralia and India.

...wth: Epiphyte with poorly
...eloped roots and two kinds of leaves.
... large flat plate-like leaves, which
...rely cover the roots, are first bright
...en, then coriaceous and brown. They
...ain on the plant after fading, and
... to form the humus on which—to a
...siderable extent—it lives. From the
...wth point between these sterile
...es, long narrow spore-bearing leaves
... formed which are shaped like the
...ers of a stag or elk, hence the name.
...er suitable conditions the fertile
...es can grow a metre (3 ft.) in length;
... are covered with whitish scales,
...are sensitive to drops of water.

Hanging plants in flower windows
facing north, warm room or shaded winter garden.

Soil: Sphagnum or shredded bark in
orchid baskets. The plant can also be
tied to a slightly rotten piece of branch
or a thick piece of bark. Peat litter,
sphagnum or rotted cow-dung may also
be packed in among the roots.

Feeding: It is not necessary to feed the
plant, but if the basic liquid fertiliser is
used, then the proportion of $\frac{1}{4}$ oz. to a
gallon is advised, and only feed once
every 3 weeks.

Water: The floury leaves will not tolerate drops of water or direct watering.
The plant containers or covering leaves
must therefore be dipped into a vessel of
warm water without moistening the fertile leaves.

Light: As for other types of ferns.

Heat: High room temperature; winter,
not below minimum 12° C. (55° F.).

Air: Will stand quite dry room air, but
no draught.

Re-potting: Generally unnecessary.

Pteris cretica

Habitat: Mediterranean countries.

Growth: Unevenly divided leaves, with
sporangia along the edge of their undersides.

Use: Particularly reliable and straight-
forward indoor plant.

Culture: Makes no great demands on
care and growth conditions. Growth
may frequently be so vigorous as to
require replanting once or twice a year

Nephrolepis exaltata

Pteris cretica

in larger pots. Winter temperatures not below minimum 10° C. (50° F.).

Variant: Albo-lineata, with pale stripes on its leaves.

Auracariaceae

Auracaria excelsa (3)

Norfolk Island Pine

Habitat: Norfolk Islands, between Australia and New Zealand, hence its name.

Growth: An evergreen conifer of pyramidal habit, with the branches radiating horizontally in groups of 5 to each tier.

Use: Good indoor plant in a cool, airy and shaded spot. Requires plenty of space on all sides, so that the branches are not deflected. ,

Soil: Acid loam with peat or pine leaf-mould.

Feeding: 2 grams of ammonium sulphate per litre ($\frac{1}{2}$ oz. per gallon) every three weeks (March–August).

Water: Plenty of water during the summer; must never be allowed to dry out. In winter, the pot soil should be kept slightly damp. Use rainwater or any other soft water. Grows well in plastic pots.

Light: Gentle shade the whole year round. May be allowed to spend the summer out of doors in the shade of

trees. If too strongly shaded during t winter, the bottom leaves turn yell and fall off.

Heat: Cool the whole year round; w ter, best at minimum 14° C. (60° F.).

Air: Gentle breeze when the new sho come through in the spring. Otherwi dry indoor air.

Re-potting: Older plants, every 3 ye in the spring.

Cutting: Top shoots must not removed, since if a tier of branch disappears, no replacement is formed.

Propagation: By taking cuttings of shoots in specialised nurseries, example in Belgium. When the s shoots are rooted, they will retain th horizontal growth. Propagation imp sible indoors.

Pest: Mealy Bug.

NOTE: Arrange for growth in cool, a and shaded spot, acid soil and rain wa Never allow the pot soil to dry up.

Cyperaceae

Cyperus alternifolius

Umbrella Plant

Habitat: Swampy terrain Madagascar. Closely related Papyrus, *Cyperus papyrus*, which used by the Ancient Egyptians for m ing paper.

Growth: Stems measuring 30–70 ($1–2\frac{1}{2}$ ft.), ending in a crown of slen leaves radiating outwards like the rib a parasol. In the spring, a circle brownish-green blooms grows above crown of leaves.

Use: Good indoor plant, which sh always stand in water. Growth pe March–September.

Soil: Soilless mixture, mixed with or ary garden soil and sand. pH 7. I tips turn brown in very acid or alkaline soil.

Feeding: 2 grams per litre ($\frac{3}{4}$ oz. gallon) every week (April–August).

Water: Grows well in a vessel of w

d must in any case always have plenty
' water. Avoid limey tap water or
utralise it with 1 gram of ammonium
lphate per litre ($\frac{1}{4}$ oz. per gallon). The
ater in the base dish or pot should not
: changed but replenished as it is used
evaporates. Remember to keep water
the base dish throughout the summer.
ght: Full sunlight or moderate shade,
, in windows facing in any direction.
eat: Usual room temperature; winter,
t below minimum 10° C. (50° F.).
r: Damp air, frequent spraying in dry
loor air.
-potting: March–July.
tting: Withered leaf shoots should be
moved from the base. Older plants
ay be cut down completely.
opagation: By division of older
ants. Leaf cuttings can be taken by
tting off a leaf with a 1-cm. ($\frac{1}{2}$-in)
m, and allowing this to float on the
face of a dish filled with water at a
nimum temperature of 20° C.
°F.). Small plants will develop in the
ds, and can be planted in small pots
h damp sand, where they will rapidly
ke roots.

rpus cernuus

bitat: Swamp terrain in the East
ies.
wth: Grassy marsh plant with thick

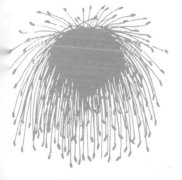

Scirpus cernuus

tussocks of dark, shiny triangular straws
which hang out over the edges of the pots,
giving the impression of a wig. During
the summer, small brownish-green
flowers appear at the tips of the straws.
Use: Good indoor plant which, as for
Cyperus alternifolius, should stand in
water. Grows best in plastic pots with
water in base dishes.
Soil: Soilless mixture.
Feeding: 2 grams per litre ($\frac{3}{4}$ oz. per
gallon) every 2 weeks (March–
September).
Water: There should always be water in
the base dish, preferably rainwater or
some other lime-free water.
Light: Not direct sunlight.
Heat: Normal room temperature.
Air: The leaves acquire brown tips in
dry indoor air, thus frequent spraying is
necessary.
Re-potting: February. The innermost
shoots grow yellow on older plants;
rejuvenate by division and by cutting
out of withered shoots.
Propagation: By division.
Pest: Red spider mite.

Gramineae

Oplismenus imbecilis
'Variegatus' (5)

Habitat: Tropics.
Growth: Up to 50 cm. (20 in.) in length,
hanging shoots with narrow leaves
striped longitudinally with green, pink
or white. Superficial appearance similar
to *Tradescantia*. Only the older,
exhausted plants produce flowers, which
are not particularly decorative.
Use: Good, undemanding plants in
warm rooms. Young plants are most
attractive, and for this reason cuttings
should be taken from the top shoots
each year and the old plants discarded.
Soil: Humus-rich loam or soilless mixture.
Feeding: 3 grams per litre (1 oz. per
gallon) every week (March–October),

otherwise the leaf tips become scorched and turn yellow and discoloured. Avoid wetting the leaves when feeding.

Water: Plenty of water in the summer and spring; moderate amounts in winter.

Light: Well-lit spot for growth, especially during the winter.

Heat: Normal room temperature; winter, not below minimum 10° C. (50° F.).

Air: Grows well in dry, indoor air. During propagation by grafting, needs more humid air.

Re-potting: Not usually worth while. Plants may instead be rejuvenated by putting cuttings of top shoots in March straight into flower-pots filled with soilless mixture mixed with sand, in a sealed atmosphere under glass or a plastic hood.

Pests: Greenfly, red spider mite.

Pandanaceae

Pandanus veitchii

Screw Pine

Habitat: Polynesia.

Growth: Excellent decorative plant, which has the appearance of a palm tree without a trunk. The narrow, pointed, metre-length (3-ft.) leaves are dark green with white edges. The individual leaves appear in the rosette in screw-thread or spiral formation around the plant's central axis, while the leaf tips have point thorns. Older plants develop buttres roots, which 'jack up' the plant from th earth, so that it has 'stilts' to stand upo Small plants often develop on the aeri roots.

Use: Undemanding indoor plant, whic however, may grow too big under no mal conditions. Older specimens may discarded and replaced with small, mo decorative, new plants.

Soil: Soilless mixture.

Feeding: 3 grams per litre (1 oz. p gallon) every 2 weeks (March–Octobe

Water: Plenty of water in spring a summer; moderate amounts in winter.

Light: Best in the half-shade. Never windows facing south.

Heat: Growth period, summer at mi mum 20–25° C. (70–80° F.). Wint slightly cooler. Growth ceases at te peratures below minimum 15° (60° F.).

Air: Dry indoor air with spraying d ing summer.

Re-potting: March; pots should not too small.

Propagation: Cut side shoots, wh often form roots while they are on parent plant.

NOTE: Often grows too big for an ind plant. Best in a conservatory. Take c with the pointed thorns.

Other species: See below.

Pandanus sanderi

Habitat: Solomon Islands.

Growth: Dark green leaves with yel stripes.

Use and culture: As for *Pandanus* chii.

Pandanus utilis

Habitat: Madagascar.

Growth: Bluish-green leaves with dish-brown thorns at the edges.

Use and culture: As for *Pandanus* chii.

Pandanus veitchii

almae

alms

abitat: The palm family includes over)00 tropical and sub-tropical varieties om all parts of the world.

rowth: Palms are elegant foliage- ants, often having elegantly dissected aves with or without trunks.

se: Only the smaller varieties are suit- le as indoor plants. Older plants, on e other hand, often become too large r indoor culture and must be moved to conservatory or greenhouse. Seldom wer in indoor culture. Palms grow the hole year round without any real rest riod, and for this reason the culture re- irements are more or less the same all e year, regulated according to quantity light and temperature. All palms ve certain cultural requirements in mmon, which are described below; any ccial cultural requirements are men- ned with the individual species.

il: Soilless mixture or well-drained nus soil, pH 5–6·5 (i.e. slightly acid).

eding: 2 grams per litre (¾ oz. per lon) every week (March–October), only after prior watering.

ater: Plenty of water during the sum- r, otherwise moderate quantities. The l balls must never be allowed to dry completely.

ht: Windows facing east or west; no ect sunlight.

at: Normal room temperature. Mini- m temperature 18° C. (65° F.) for the es requiring most heat; for the re nder, minimum 15° C. (60° F.).

: Frequent syringing to increase air idity.

potting: Every spring, February– rch. Older plants, on the other hand, ry two or three years. Use deep, nar- pots, so that the aerial roots are not high. Planting should be very firm; the soil in carefully around the es.

pagation: Seeding may be successful ors. Soil temperature approximate

minimum 30° C. (85° F.). The seeds may remain in the soil for several months before the shoots become visible.

Pests: Scale insects, mealy bug, red spider mites and thrips, especially when plants are placed in warm or sunlit posi- tions.

Varieties: See below.

Chamaedorea elegans (*syn* Neanthe bella)

Habitat: Mexico.

Growth: Hardy dwarf palm with lobed leaves, having 20-cm. (7-in.) long small leaves. The stem, which develops over the years, is of the thickness of a finger, smooth, with bracts behind the leaves, which later fall away. Even small plants in 10-cm. (3½-in.) pots form rather insignificant green inflorescences and subsequently exciting, colourful fruit clusters.

Special cultural requirements: A lot of water, also in base dish. High tempera- ture: winter, not below minimum 12° C. (55° F.). For other requirements, see under *Palms*.

Chamaerops humilis

Habitat: Mediterranean countries. Only wild palm in Europe.

Chamaerops humilis

Microcoelum weddelianum

Growth: Stems grow up to a metre (3 ft.) in height, developing first in older plants. The leaves are fan-shaped, with spiny stems.
Special cultural requirements: May be left to spend the summer on a balcony, terrace, or in a patio. Minimum temperature in winter 5° C. (40° F.). In a well-lit place. Other cultural requirements, see under *Palms*.

Microcoelum weddelianum (*syn* Cocos weddelliana)

Known in the United States as Microcoelum mortianum

Habitat: Brazil.
Growth: Smallest, but most decorative of all indoor palms. Has elegant, feather-like leaves. Sold as small plants, and can only be kept in a room for a few years.
Special cultural requirements: Plenty of water, best with permanent water in a base dish. High wintering temperature, at least 18° C. (65° F.). Other cultural requirements, see under *Palms*.

Howea belmoreana   (6)

Kentia Palm

Habitat: Howe Islands in the Pacific, the capital of which is called Kentia, hence also the name *Kentia belmoreana*.
Growth: Very broad and sturdy lobed leaves with wide pendulous leaflets.

Special cultural requirements: Impose no great demands, but should not be exposed to too harsh sunlight. Best winter temperature, minimum 14–18° C (55–65° F.). For other cultural requirements, see under *Palms*.

Phoenix canariensis

Habitat: Canary Islands.
Growth: Strong-growing plant, with large, feather-like leaves.
Special cultural requirements: Good to plant to be placed out of doors in the sun during summer. Winter cool temperature, but not below minimum 5°C (40° F.). For other cultural requirements, see under *Palms*.

Phoenix dactylifera

Date Palm

Habitat: Tropics.
Growth: Very vigorous grower with stiff, prickly leaves. After 10–15 years becomes too big as an indoor plant but suitable for a conservatory.
Cultural requirements: See under *Palms*.
Propagation: May be propagated by seeding in ordinary moist soil. For the first year, the palm consists only of a single grass-like leaf.

Phoenix dactylifera

oenix roebelinii

abitat: East Indies.
owth: Sturdy, undemanding indoor
nt with slow growth.
ecial cultural requirements:
nimum temperature in winter 15° C.
)° F.). For other cultural require-
nts, see under *Palms.*

aceae

laonema pseudobracteatum   (7)

bitat: Malaya.
owth: Foliage plant with pointed,
al leaves, with white central vein and
ite and yellow markings. Height 40
. (16 in.). Flowers have no orna-
ntal value. More durable than
ffenbachia, which has a tendency to
d its lower leaves in indoor culture.
e: Quite a demanding indoor plant.
ll not be squeezed in between other
nts, and does not take kindly to being
ved. Only lasts a few years in indoor
ture.
l: Light humus soil mixed with sand,
possibly soilless mixture. The roots
:lose to the surface of the soil, and it
st therefore be planted in wide, flat
s.
ding: 2 grams per litre ($\frac{3}{4}$ oz. per
on) every 2 weeks (February–July).
ter: Always keep the soil moist; does
stand drying out.
ht: Shade, never direct sunlight.
ives well in dark entrance halls or
rcases. Best in windows facing east,
t or north.
t: Likes a warm spot. In a shaded
tion, the winter temperature can be
ow as 15° C. (60° F.) minimum, but
erwise warmer.
Stands up to dry air. In very warm
ospheres, however, needs frequent
nging.
otting: February, in pans rather
 pots.
s: Mealy bug, red spider mite.
er species: See below.

Aglaonema costatum

Growth: Pointed, oval leaves, with white
central vein and white spots. Height
20 cm. (8 in.).
Use and culture: As for *Aglaonema
pseudobracteatum.*

Aglaonema modestum

Growth: Unvariegated green leaves.
Height 30 cm. (1 ft.).
Use and culture: As for *Aglaonema
pseudobracteatum.*

Aglaonema roebelinii

Growth: Broad, oval leaves, with conspicuous silver-grey markings on the
otherwise dark green surface of the leaf.
Height 40 cm. (16 in.).
Use and culture: As for *Aglaonema
pseudobracteatum.*

Aglaonema oblongifolium curtisii

Growth: Narrow, oval-pointed dark
green leaves with silvery side veins.
Height 40 cm. (16 in.). The sturdiest of
the *Aglaonema* varieties.
Use and culture: As for *Aglaonema
pseudobracteatum.*

Anthurium scherzerianum   (8)

Flamingo Flower

Habitat: Guatemala.
Growth: The leaf and flower stems shoot
forth from the necks of the roots at the
surface of the soil. The leaves are narrow and dark green in colour, and have
long stems. The small yellow flowers are
gathered into a dense spike or spadix,
reminiscent of a pig's tail; this spike is
surrounded by a scarlet, pale red or
white spathe, which persists for several
months.
Use: Durable and decorative indoor
plant, which has a preference for warm,

153

humid air but thrives surprisingly well in an ordinary room atmosphere.

Soil: Very light, porous mixture, e.g. soilless mixture and sand. Bracken peat and leaf mould with charcoal added is also a good mixture.

Feeding: 6 grams per litre (2 oz. per gallon) every 3 weeks (February–December), but apply only when the soil ball is already moist. Roots are sensitive to too high a concentration of salts in the soil; it will therefore be an advantage to use an organic fertiliser (such as cowdung) alternately with artificial fertiliser.

Water: The light porous mixture dries out quickly and, since the plant is damaged if allowed to dry out even once, frequent watering is an unbreakable rule. The best method is to dip the entire pot into lukewarm water. Rainwater is to be preferred.

Light: Half or full shade. Will not tolerate direct sunlight.

Heat: Winter not below a minimum 15° C. (60° F.).

Air: Moist air with frequent syringing.

Re-potting: Early spring, when the necks of the roots have pushed themselves up over the surface of the soil, in wide, flat pots with plenty of room for the roots. Never plant too deeply.

Diseases: Brown edges on the leaves when the soil or air is too dry, and the light too harsh. Avoid calcium deposits on leaves when watering.

Other species: See below.

Anthurium crystallinum   (9)

Habitat: Peru.

Growth: Handsome foliage plant with very large, velvety, olive-green leaves having silvery-white veins.

Use: Best in very warm greenhouse or conservatory. Uncertain in room culture.

Culture: Similar to *Anthurium scherzerianum*, but requires higher temperatures and higher degree of air humidity.

Dieffenbachia picta   (1

Dumb Cane

Habitat: Tropical America.

Growth: Sturdy, erect trunk with cl green leaves on long stems with dots a blotches in white, pale yellow and p green. Cultivated as a young plant a discarded when the bottom leaves shed, its value as an ornamental plan thus debatable.

Use: Best in a warm greenhouse, also good in a room after careful h dening off. Thrives for a time in d shade. Requires a lot of space.

Soil: Soilless mixture or light leaf mo with peat added.

Feeding: 3 grams per litre (1 oz. gallon) every week (March–October).

Water: Should be kept moist all the y round. Will not stand drying out.

Light: Never direct sunlight. Thrive shady rooms, halls or staircases.

Heat: Poor growth if temperature f below minimum 15° C. (60° F.) dur winter.

Air: Frequent spraying, especially summer.

Re-potting: Every spring, in spaci pots.

Propagation: By cuttings in a gr house in an enclosed atmosphere, bottom heat.

Pests: Mealy bug, red spider n especially when the growing poin too brightly lit.

NOTE: The sap in the leaves and stem poisonous.

Other varieties: There are many hyb between this and other species wi great variation in the distribution colours in the leaves. See also below

Dieffenbachia leopoldii

Growth: Very popular *Dieffenba* species with plain green leaves.

Use and culture: As for *Dieffenba picta*.

154

onstera deliciosa (12)

ibitat: Tropical swamps in Mexico.
owth: Sturdy climbing plant; the large
ield-like leaves have lobed in-
ions and holes. From the stems, large
nches of hanging aerial roots are
med. Older plants may, under favour-
le conditions in conservatories or
thouses, develop large, calla-like
lorescences with white spathes. Later,
matic edible fruits appear, which
ve a taste similar to that of a pine-
ple.
e: Decorative room plant, requiring a
of space. Suitable for trellising to
lls, doorways and large windows.
il: Soilless mixture, or garden soil
h added peat. pH 6·5.
ding: 3 grams per litre (1 oz. per
lon) every week (March—October).
tiliser should only be applied to
ist soil.
ter: Plenty in the summer, moderate
ount in the winter.
ht: Shade or half-shade. In brightly
positions, the leaves acquire brown
ts and edges.
at: Normal room temperature, but
less than 12°C. (55°F.).
: Syringe during growth. Will stand
to very good centrally heated air.
notting: Every 3 or 4 years.
pagation: By cutting top shoots with
aerial roots attached. They should
lanted in equal parts of soilless mix-
and sand, and must be kept moist
warm.
ieties: borsigiana (but correctly
nstera pertusa), which has smaller
es and more aerial roots than the
, and grows more rapidly and vigor-
y. Can also be used in smaller
ns. This is the variety illustrated.
E: Aerial roots, which—like ordin-
roots—serve as ducts for transmit-
water and nourishment, must not be
oved. They can be trained down into
sc dish which is permanently filled
water in order to facilitate the

plant's growth. Deficiency of 'window
holes' in the leaves is the result of too
little water and nourishment and too
dark a growth position.

Philodendron scandens

Sweetheart Vine

Habitat: West Indies.
Growth: Vigorous climbing plant (liana)
with pointed, heart-shaped leaves which
—while very small on young plants—
grow to lengths of 30 cm. (1 ft.) on older
specimens. New leaves are reddish-
brown and almost transparent.
Use: Well suited as climbing plants on
trellises or walls or as a hanging-basket
plant, also as a ground covering in conservatories. An amusing method of culture is to allow the plant to grow up a
stick enveloped in moist moss or sphagnum. Good for shady situations. One of
our most attractive and hardiest indoor
plants.
Soil: Soilless mixture.
Feeding: 3 grams per litre (1 oz. per
gallon) every week (March—September).
Water: Summer, plentiful; winter,
moderate.

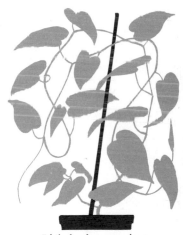

Philodendron scandens

Philodendron erubescens

Light: Easily satisfied, does not stand direct sunshine.

Heat: Normal room temperature; not less than 12°C. (55°F.). Avoid violent fluctuations of temperature.

Air: Syringing when room temperature is high.

Re-potting: Spring, in pots which must not be too large.

Propagation: By cuttings with aerial roots, as for *Monstera deliciosa*.

Other species: See below.

Philodendron erubescens

Growth: Vigorous climbing plant with dark red markings on the leaf stems, and glistening dark green leaves with red edges and undersides. The young leaves are a coppery colour. Older plants produce a number of dark, copper-coloured flowers.

Use and culture: As for *Philodendron scandens*, and is as easily satisfied.

Philodendron ilsemannii

Growth: Climbing plant with variegated leaves and slow-growing stems. The lancet-shaped dark green leaves have irregular white markings. The variegated patterns disappear in poor light conditions.

Use and culture: As for *Philodendr* *scandens.* Considerably less hardy.

Philodendron bipinnatifidum

Growth: Vigorous foliage plant with climbing stems. The body of the leaf 50 cm. (20 in.) long and feathered; leaf stems are also 50 cm. (20 in.) lo and hollow. The leaves sprout from central growing point.

Use: Requires a lot of space; theref best in a conservatory.

Culture: As for *Philodendron scande.*

Philodendron melanochrysum (*t* is the juvenile form of andreanum)

Growth: The most decorative of Philodendron species. The leav shaped like arrow shafts hanging ve cally and overlapping, are dark gr with shades of copper and pale yel veins. They grow to 80 cm. (32 in.) electric light the leaves look as if t are covered with gold dust.

Use and culture: As for *Philodend* *scandens*, but needs higher temp tures—not below 18°C. (65°F.) m mum—and greater air humidity frequent syringing and more water.

Philodendron melanochrysum

uromatum venosum (guttatum)

onarch of the East

abitat: East Indies.

owth: Odd plant with a large tuber, m which first the flower and later the ves emerge, without culture in soil or ter being necessary. The flower is sur- inded by an olive-green spathe with rplish-brown markings, and when ly developed gives off a disgusting rion smell. The leaves are deeply cut l very decorative.

e: In the early spring, the dry tuber is ced in a warm, dry spot without ect sunlight. Flowering period, oruary–March. After this the tuber is ted and the plant watered and looked er in the normal way, while the leaves ture. In October the top withers away in. May be put out of doors for the imer but must be taken in before the : night frost. To be kept dry through the winter at minimum 10°C. °F.).

l: Light loam with sand added.

ding: 5 grams per litre (1¼ oz. per on) every week during growth, until es begin to wither.

er: Plentiful in summer, to be kept from October.

ht: Half-shade.

Scindapsus aureus

Heat: Normal room temperature; winter not less than minimum 10°C. (50°F.).

Air: Dry indoor air during flowering. During leaf period, frequent syringing.

Re potting: Potting after flowering is finished. The tuber is covered with 3 cm. (1¼ in.) of soil.

NOTE: The smell of the withering flower is particularly unpleasant.

Scindapsus aureus

Habitat: East Indies, New Guinea and the Solomon Islands.

Growth: Hanging or climbing plant with longish, symmetrical, fresh green leaves with yellow patterns. The young shoots and leaf stems are yellowish.

Use: Very suitable as a hanging or climbing plant in very shaded situations.

Soil: Light humus soil or standard potting mixture.

Feeding: 3 grams per litre (1 oz. per gallon) every week (March–October).

Water: Soil should be evenly moist in

Sauromatum venosum

summer but never thoroughly wet. Winter, better too dry than too damp.

Light: Imposes no great demands. At high room temperatures, however, during winter, the growth position should be as well-lit as possible.

Heat: Normal room temperature during winter; not less than minimum 15° C. (60° F.).

Air: Frequent sprinkling during summer.

Re-potting: February–May, when growth begins.

Propagation: Cuttings from sections of stems with aerial roots are potted in sand and sphagnum. Keep close until roots have begun to develop.

Other species: See below.

Scindapsus pictus

Growth: Heart-shaped dark green leaves with small silver markings.

Use and culture: As for *Scindapsus aureus.*

Variant: argyraeus, with black-green leaves having silvery-white markings and edges. Well suited for trellising against as dark as possible a background, which may set off the characteristic leaves. Requires more warmth and greater air humidity than the type.

Spathiphyllum patinii (*syn* kochii, wallisii *of nurserymen*) (13)

White Sails

Habitat: Tropical America.

Growth: Smooth, dark green leaves on long stems, from a horizontal root stock. The spadix-shaped inflorescence is yellowish-white, the open spathe pure white. After flowering has finished, the seed cluster and enveloping leaf changes to green. Long-lasting flowers in spring or early summer (often has a second flowering in the autumn).

Use: Sturdy indoor plant in a very da room. Decorative as a fresh folia plant outside the flowering season.

Soil: Soilless mixture.

Feeding: 2 grams per litre ($\frac{3}{4}$ oz. gallon) every 2 weeks (Marc September), but only on to damp s Too much fertiliser produces brown l tips.

Water: Summer, constant soil moistu winter, moderate watering.

Light: Very easily satisfied; very s able for windows facing north.

Heat: Normal room temperature; wir not less than minimum 15° C. (60° F

Air: Tolerates dry room air.

Re-potting: February–March.

Propagation: By division during potting.

Diseases: One of the healthiest ind plants.

Syngonium auritum

Habitat: Tropical America.

Growth: Vigorous climbing plant dark green 3- or 5-fingered leaves ing spear-shaped lobes.

Use: Easily cultivated climbing pl for trellises or moss-covered rods. G in the shade, in rooms which are not cool.

Soil: Soilless mixture.

Feeding: 3 grams per litre (1 oz. gallon) every week (March–Septemb

Water: Must not be allowed to dry Evenly moist soil is preferable.

Light: Half-shade or full shade, direct sunlight.

Heat: Normal room temperature; ter, not less than minimum 15 (60° F.).

Air: Thrives in very dry room air.

Re-potting: Should be transpla every year in February so that gr should not be retarded.

Propagation: By taking cuttings of sections together with the aerial roo

Other species: See below.

Syngonium auritum

...gonium podophyllum

...osefoot Plant

...wth: Leaves divided into 5 or 8 sec-
...s. Of particular interest is the *albo-
...atum* form which has velvet green
...es with white stripes along the cen
... and side veins ('Emerald Gem' of
...crymen).

... *and culture:* As for *Syngonium
...tum.* (Sometimes sold under the
...e *Nephthytis.*)

...tedeschia aethiopica   (14)

...m Lily

...itat: Marshes in South Africa. Often
...d in the tropics as a luxuriant weed
...t in ditches and swamps.

...wth: Perennial, with fleshy tubers
... arrowhead-shaped leaves on suc-
...nt stalks which may grow up to a
...e (3 ft.) in height. From January to
...l the flower stalks sprout forth with
...rant yellow flower heads surrounded
... cornet-shaped white spathe.

... Decorative room plant which
...ires a great deal of space, and
...ty of water during the growth period
... July to April. Must be kept ab

solutely dry during the resting period
which is generally from May to June,
but sometimes the plants continue growing until June. May be taken from its
pot and planted out in a garden in July
once the top has almost withered. Potting in October.

Soil: Soilless mixture.

Feeding: 4 grams per litre (1¼ oz. per
gallon) every week during growth period
(July–November).

Water: Bog plant which requires plenty
of water; a good method is to have
permanent water in a base dish. Only
during the resting period (May–June)
can water be omitted altogether, so
that the pot soil can thoroughly dry
out.

Light: Tolerates a great deal of light, but
the pot with the soil ball must be
shielded from direct sunlight.

Heat: Summer, in a garden or on a balcony at normal temperatures. From
October to New Year, best at minimum
10° C. (50° F.), subsequently at minimum 15° C. (60° F.) so as to assist
flowering.

Air: Humid air with frequent syringing on hot days outside the resting
period.

Re-potting: Pot up divided plants in
large pots in October after spending the
summer out of doors.

Propagation: By division of old plants,
also in October.

Diseases: Brown edges on leaves when
plants are fed while soil is dry.

Pests: Red spider mite when kept in too
light or too dry a location.

Other species: See below.

Zantedeschia elliottiana

Growth: Green leaves with silvery-grey
markings. Clear golden-yellow flowers.

Use and culture: As for *Zantedeschia
aethiopica*, but needs somewhat higher
temperature after New Year (minimum
18° C. (65° F.)) in order to flower.

Zantedeschia elliottiana

Commelinaceae

Rhoeo discolor (*syn* spathacea) (15)

Habitat: Central America.
Growth: Stems up to 30 cm. (1 ft.) high, with lance-shaped leaves arranged in a rosette with olive-green top surfaces and blue-violet undersides. Reminiscent of *Dracaena* and *Bromelia*. The white flowers nestle in the axils, hidden in the cradle-like greenish-violet bracts, from which they just peep out during the short-lived flowering period. In America this is known as 'Moses in the Cradle'.
Use: Good foliage plant for windows facing west or east, where the atmosphere is warm and humid in summer and warm and dry in winter. Most attractive as a single plant.
Soil: Soilless mixture, or loam mixed with sand.
Feeding: 2 grams per litre ($\frac{3}{4}$ oz. per gallon) every 2 weeks (March–September).
Water: Summer, constant moisture in the soil; winter, dry so that the shoots do not rot on the surface of the soil.
Light: Shaded situation for the summer, lighter spot for winter.
Heat: Summer, normal room temperature; winter, not less than minimum 15° C. (60° F.).

Air: The leaves roll up in dry air. Spr well in summer.
Re-potting: March–June in large pots, which the plants will rapidly grow larg
Propagation: By taking cuttings of s shoots in early spring.
Variant: vittata, which has yellow a white longitudinal stripes on the leav Slower growth and more heat and li required in winter than for the type.

Tradescantia albiflora (

Wandering Jew

Habitat: Tropical America.
Growth: Creeping and hanging grow with succulent plain green leaves shoots. Flowers are in bloom from ea summer to autumn. They are white, only open for a few hours.
Use: Excellent hanging plant in v dows which are not too bright. Indif ent to fluctuations in temperature thrives at temperatures from minim 10–25° C. (50–80° F.). May be cu vated as a 'water plant' with cut runr in water. Good for cultivation in pla pots.
Soil: Soilless mixture.
Feeding: 3 grams per litre (1 oz. per lon) every 2 weeks (March–Sept ber). When too much nourishmen given, the colours of the leaves fade the more gaily-coloured varieties.
Water: The soil must always be damp, especially during summer.
Light: Half-shade or full shade, ever sunlight.
Heat: Normal room temperature; ter, not less than minimum 10 (50° F.) however.
Air: Likes humid air, but thrives we dry indoor air as long as it is g plenty of water.
Re-potting: Older plants grow spi and unattractive, and should there be discarded in favour of one-year plants.
Propagation: By cuttings of top sh in the spring, either in water followe

tting after the formation of roots, or
ectly into damp soilless mixture in
all pots with several cuttings in each.
st: Greenfly.
riant: aureovittata with irregular yel-
 stripes on the leaves.
her species: See below.

adescantia blossfeldiana

owth: Covered with thick, white fur.
 leathery leaves are green on their
er sides and red on their undersides.
 flowers are pink.
 and culture: As for Tradescantia
iflora.

descantia fluminensis

wth: Reddish violet stems, green
es with violet undersides, and white
vers in great profusion.
 and culture: As for Tradescantia
flora.
iety: albovittata with white-striped
es.

descantia navicularis

wth: Thick leaves. Grows more
ly than the other Tradescantia var
s.
 and culture: As for Tradescantia
lora. Must be kept cool and in the
during winter. Minimum tempera-
10° C. (50° F.).

rina pendula   (17)

itat: Central America and Mexico.
wth: Fast-growing hanging plant,
h can only be distinguished from
descantia by obscure botanical dif-
ces. The leaves are dark green with
silvery-white stripes on the upper
. The purplish-pink flowers emerge
e early spring.
  Hanging plant for windows facing
or west. Even growth all the year
d with no real resting period.

Soil: Standard potting mixture.
Feeding: 3 grams per litre (1 oz. per gallon) every 2 weeks (March–October). Too much nitrogen will cause the colours to fade.
Water: Summer, plenty; winter, moderate.
Light: Half or full shade; winter somewhat lighter.
Heat: Normal room temperature; winter, not below minimum 10° C. (50° F.).
Air: Preferably humid air. The leaves roll up in very dry room air.
Re-potting: Not advisable. Older plants are unattractive and should be replaced by younger ones.
Propagation: Remove top shoots in the spring and plant them, several together in each pot, in soilless compost mixed with sand. Plastic pots are very suitable.
Pests: Greenfly, snails and slugs.
Variety: quadricolor, in which the leaves, in addition to the other colours, have white and light red stripes on their upper sides.

Liliaceae

Agapanthus orientalis   (18)

African Lily

Habitat: South Africa.
Growth: Vigorous plant growing to 75 cm. (2½ ft.) long, narrow leaves and pretty blue flowers on long stems. Flowers throughout the summer.
Use: Requires a lot of space. Very suitable as a tub plant in a patio, on a terrace or a balcony. To be kept dry and cool but frost free during winter in a cellar or unheated conservatory. To assist flowering, the plant must be kept completely dry from November to the beginning of May.
Soil: Rich compost with bonemeal added. Good drainage.
Feeding: 3 grams per litre (1 oz. per gallon) every week (May–July).
Water: Must be kept well watered from May to October. After that, the water

must be given sparingly and the plant kept completely dry from November to May.

Light: Well-lit situation; may be in full sunlight. Winter, as close to daylight as possible.

Heat: Summer, normal temperature; winter, minimum 2–8° C. (38–45° F.). Will not stand frost.

Air: Spray on hot summer days.

Re-potting: See Propagation.

Propagation: Every 3 or 4 years the older plants should be divided, preferably in April. Frequent disturbance will discourage flowering. Administer basic feeding with bonemeal (Animix) on re-potting.

Pest: Greenfly.

Aloe arborescens

Habitat: South Africa.

Growth: Succulent, with upright stems and thick fleshy leaves having prickly edges. Large clusters of orange-red bell-shaped flowers.

Use: Ideal indoor plant, the growth period of which comes, in contrast to that of many other indoor plants, in the winter-time, while flowering takes place from March to July.

Soil: Loam and sand with good drainage at the base of the pot.

Feeding: 3 grams per litre (1 oz. gallon) every 2 weeks (February December).

Water: Moderate watering during growth period in winter and spring while the plant is kept relatively dry during the summer and during its rest period.

Light: Full sunlight.

Heat: Normal room temperature; summer, as cool as possible. Minimum temperature 10° C. (50° F.).

Air: Thrives best in dry air, thus well suited for centrally heated rooms. Avoid excessive moisture on the plant, which might cause the stem to rot.

Re-potting: At intervals of several years in pots which are not too large, after flowering has ceased in July–August.

Propagation: By side shoots or leaf cuttings, the cut surface of which must be allowed to dry before they are planted in soil with a generous amount of sand added.

Diseases: Tendency to rot if watered too heavily or if the degree of air humidity is too high.

Other species: See below.

Aloe variegata

Partridge-breasted Aloe

Growth: Triangular leaves with white markings, arranged in a distinct cross pattern, and a white prickly edge. The flowers are large and orange-red with drops of pleasant-tasting nectar.

Use and culture: As for *Aloe arborescens*.

NOTE: Will not tolerate water in the rosette.

Asparagus sprengeri

Habitat: Natal.

Growth: Thin, trailing branches with narrow needle-like leaves. Older plants develop thorns. The plant must be

Aloe arborescens

ntly rejuvenated by cutting away old
oots.

e: Good plant for hanging bowls,
en under poor conditions. Thrives in
drained flower-pots. Will stand either
rm or cold wintering, and omission of
ting period which is October–March.
commercial nurseries, this and—even
re—the following species are exten-
ely used as greenery for bouquets of
wers

il: Soilless compost mixture or
nus-rich loam with pH 6·5.

ding: 5 grams per litre (1½ oz. per
lon) every week (March–August).

ter: During growth period, plenty of
ter, but must be kept drier during the
tcr. The swollen tubers protect it
m drying out.

ht: Light, sunny place. Does not like
de or dark rooms, which cause small
discoloured leaves.

at: Summer, normal room tem-
ature; winter, minimum 12–20° C.
–70° F.) in a well-lit growing posi-
.

 When the resting period ends in
ruary the plant likes humid air with
uent sprinkling. Otherwise dry room

otting: February, in large pots, as
roots require a lot of space.

oagation: By division of old plants,
rwise by seed.

s: Greenfly, with too much heat in
spring. Do not spray with nicotine,
ch scorches the plant, but use
lasect or something similar.

ases: Small leaves are shed when
e is a lack of light or when the tem-
ture fluctuates too sharply.

er species: See below.

aragus plumosus

aragus Fern

wth: Pretty indoor plant with very
y divided foliage. The variety *com-
us* can be used as a house plant.
ers readily and grows pretty red

Asparagus plumosus

berries.* Produces fresh shoots when-
ever pruned. Best plant for cut greenery.
Use and culture: As for *Asparagus
sprengeri*, but somewhat more difficult
indoors since it will not tolerate warm,
dry air during the winter. Prefers cool,
humid air and slight shade.

Aspidistra elatior

Habitat: Southern Japan.
Growth: Broad, lancet-shaped leaves
sprout like gigantic Lily of the Valley
leaves from the thick, fleshy root stocks.
Unattractive, brownish-violet flowers
right on the surface of the soil.
Use: One of our most easily satisfied
indoor plants, which thrives even in the
darkest corner of the room. Ideal for
stairways and as a 'restaurant plant'.
Soil: Soilless mixture.
Feeding: In summer, 3 grams per litre (1
oz. per gallon) every 2 weeks, but only
on moist soil.
Water: Summer, moderate watering;
winter, less.
Light: Will stand deep shade, but better
growth in a lighter place in a window
facing north, north-west or north-east.

* But the plant is dioecious and plants of
both sexes are necessary.

Aspidistra elatior

Heat: Normal room temperature.
Air: Will stand dry room air, but much better growth in humid air.
Re-potting: Every 2 or 3 years in pots which are not too large.
Propagation: By division on re-potting. Root stocks must be cut through with a sharp knife, so that there are 2–3 leaves on each rhizome.
Pest: Snails or slugs on new leaves.

Chlorophytum comosum variegatum   (20)

Spider Plant

Habitat: South Africa.
Growth: The name Spider Plant refers to the long flower stems which, at a considerable distance from the parent plant, produce new plants which strike roots. Leaves are long, narrow and grass-like. The flowers small, white stars on yellow stems.
Use: Undemanding plant for hanging bowls. Older plants with a great many flower stems and new leaf-rosettes are very decorative.
Soil: Soilless mixture. Thrives particularly well in plastic pots.
Feeding: 2 grams per litre ($\frac{3}{4}$ oz. per gallon) every week (March–October).
Water: Plenty of water from February to September, otherwise quite dry.

Light: Half-shade. During the winter close to a window as possible.
Heat: Equally suitable for cool a warm rooms.
Air: Spray during the summertime; w stand dry room air otherwise.
Re-potting: Spring or summer. T vigorous, fleshy roots will push the pla up out of the pot, if the latter is too li and too narrow; for this reason, u large, wide pots.
Propagation: Small plants are cut fr the flower stems and planted in soill mixture mixed with sand.
Diseases: Brown leaf tips are a sign feeding when too dry.
Variety: 'Variegatum' with a bro white centre line along the central v of the leaf. More decorative than green type.

Cordyline australis

Habitat: New Zealand.
Growth: Roots white. Stem low v swollen root stock and a thick ros 100 cm. (3 ft.) long and 20 cm. (8 broad, sword-shaped, coriaceous lea with light green central vein. The w flower tufts appear from March to M
Use: Ornamental plant for conser tories, but too big as a room plant.
Soil: Soilless mixture or potting c post.
Feeding: 3 grams per litre (1 oz. gallon) every 2 weeks (April–Octobe
Water: Summer, plentiful; win moderate. Will stand extended peri of drought.
Light: Well-lit, sunny situation.
Heat: May be kept out of doors du summer, on a terrace or balco Should be kept free from frost and v lit during winter.
Air: Will stand dry air.
Re-potting: Every 2 years in the spr Avoid damaging the thick, fleshy roo
Pruning: The top can be cut of autumn or spring, which will resu several crowns being formed.

opagation: By seed.
st: Scale insect.
her species: See below.

ordyline indivisa

owth: Like *Cordyline australis*, but
th smaller leaves which have red cen-
l veins. Otherwise use and cultivate in
e same way.

ordyline terminalis

owth: Leaves 50 cm. (18 in.) long and
cm. (4 in.) wide on stems. There are
ieties with leaves in varying shades
red. Spreads branches easily.
e and culture: As for *Cordyline*
tralia, but must spend the winter in a
ted room at minimum 15–18° C.
–65° F.).
ting: The top can be removed to
uce branching.
pagation: By cuttings of top shoots
base heat of minimum 25° C.
° F.).

acaena draco

bit: Difficult to distinguish from
dyline, but it has orange-red roots
stems which are not swollen. The
es are narrow, stiff and green.

Cordyline terminalis

Use: Young plants indoors; older ones,
because of their size, best in a conserva-
tory or greenhouse.
Soil: Light humus-rich loam or soilless
mixture.
Feeding: 3 grams per litre (1 oz. per
gallon) every 2 weeks (March–
September).
Water: Moderate watering, but during
winter should be kept quite dry.
Light: Half-shade or light.
Heat: In summer can be kept out of
doors; winter, not below minimum
10° C. (50° F.).
Air: Will stand dry air.
Re-potting: From time to time during
spring in pots which are not too large.
Propagation: By seed.
Pests. Scale insect, red spider mite.
Other species: See below.

Dracaena deremensis   (21)

Habitat: Tropical Africa.
Growth: Upright, with leaves 30 cm. (18
in.) long.
Use and culture: As for *Dracaena
draco,* but requires higher temperatures;
winter not below minimum 15° C.
(60° F.).
Propagation: By cuttings.
Varieties: bausei, with a broad white
central stripe along the central vein of
the leaf, and *warneckii* with a number of
narrow, white longitudinal stripes on the
leaves.

Dracaena fragrans

Habitat: Tropical Africa.
Growth: Very broad, succulent leaves
50 cm. (20 in.) long, gathered into a
rosette. Fragrant, white flowers coming
from the axils.
Use and culture: As for *Dracaena
draco,* but requires higher temperatures;
winter, not below minimum 18° C.
(65° F.). Just as undemanding with
regard to light as *Aspidistra.*
Propagation: By cuttings.

Varieties: massangeana, which has leaves with a yellow central stripe, and *lindenii*, with leaves having broad, yellow strips along their edges.

Dracaena godseffiana

Habitat: Tropical Africa.
Growth: Thin stems with small, round, green leaves which have yellow dots. (The 'Florida Beauty' has particularly marked dots.) Growth is weak, which is why 3—5 plants are frequently planted together in one pot.
Use and culture: As for *Dracaena draco*, but requires higher temperatures; winter, not below minimum 18° C. (65° F.).

Dracaena marginata   (22)

Habitat: Madagascar.
Growth: Narrow leaves 50 cm. (20 in.) long, with red edges.
Use and culture: As for *Dracaena draco*, but requires higher temperature; winter, not below minimum 18° C. (65° F.).

Dracaena sanderiana

Habitat: Tropical Africa.
Growth: Upright stems, with yellow-and-white-striped, lance-shaped leaves. Weak growth, which is why several plants should be planted in the same pot.
Use and culture: As for *Dracaena draco*, but requires higher temperature; winter, not below minimum 18° C. (65° F.).
[In England, 13° C. (55° F.) is quite sufficient for the last 4 species.]

Gasteria verrucosa

Habitat: South Africa.
Growth: Succulent, reminiscent of *Aloe*. The fleshy leaves grow opposite one

Gasteria verrucosa

another in two rows and are cove with dense, white spots and warts. L flower stems with urn-shaped, oran red flowers, spring or summer.
Use: Ideal indoor plant. Thrives in c trally heated rooms and even in full s light in windows facing south.
Soil: Loam mixed with sand, and p sibly soilless mixture.
Feeding: 2 grams per litre ($\frac{3}{4}$ oz. gallon) every 3 weeks (March—July).
Water: Only completely dry pla should be watered. Infrequent wate during winter. Dry plants winter bes cool rooms.
Light: Well-lit, sunny spot for growt
Heat: Airy place during summer; ter, best at 6—8° C. (40—45° F.).
Air: Will stand dry air outstandi well.
Re-potting: February, or after flowe has ended in June.
Propagation: By division or by cutt of side shoots in February.
Diseases: When kept out of doors ing summer in strong sunshine, le will turn brown. With too much m ture during winter, the plant may ro

Haworthia margaritifera

Habitat: South Africa.
Growth: Succulent with a pretty, rosette, which when looked at f above is somewhat like a starfish. leaves are dark green and thi covered with white spots. Long, flower stems in spring, with a numb small bell-shaped, whitish flowers.

se: Ideal indoor plant in full sunlight
d dry air.
il: Loam mixed with sand or soilless
xture.
eding: 2 grams per litre ($\frac{3}{4}$ oz. per
llon) every 4 weeks (April–August).
ater: Summer, normal watering; win-
, more sparingly, but the soil ball
ust never be allowed to dry out com-
tely.
ght: Full sunlight in windows facing
uth.
at: Summer, in an airy location; win-
, minimum 12° C. (54° F.).
-potting: February, or after flowering
s ceased in June, in flat pots.
opagation: The side shoots can be cut
re-potting and planted on their own.
TE: Requires higher temperature and
re moisture than its close relatives,
e and *Gasteria.*

acinthus orientalis   (23)

acinth

bitat: Asia Minor.
owth: Vigorous, perennial bulb with
row leaves and flower stems bearing
rge number of bell-shaped flowers.
: Bulb growth from the garden,
ich may be forced to some advantage
lower-pots or boxes with light garden
'Water culture' in bulb glasses is,
wever, easier. The first hyacinths can
brought into bloom at Christmas-
e. By taking the bulbs indoors at
rvals of a few weeks each time, it is
ssible to have flowers right through to
rch–April.
: Normal garden soil mixed with
d, or possibly soilless mixture (which
s admirably in England), or pure
er in a bulb glass.
ding: Unnecessary, since the plant
ains its nourishment from the bulb,
if fed the bulbs will maintain their
our.
er: The bulb must not be allowed to
up once during forcing. If this hap-
, the roots may die or become

scorched, and the plant may fail to
flower.
Light: The spike must be kept dark with
a black plastic sheet or a paper hood,
which should remain in position until
the bud emerges above the leaves. If
light reaches the spike too early, the
flowers may unfold down among the
leaves and the stem will not elongate.
Heat: When forcing is started, as cool
as possible, to correspond with natural
conditions of wintering out of doors in
the soil, not more than 9° C. (48° F.).
When the spike is 5 cm. (2 in.) long, the
bulb may be taken into room heat.
When the flowers have emerged the
atmosphere should be cooler once more
in order to prolong the flowering period.
Pre-treated ('prepared') bulbs may be
forced straight away in normal room
temperatures.
Air: Will stand dry room air, but the soil
must be kept moist.
Suggestion for forcing in flower-pots:
The bulb is placed in a pot of loam
mixed with sand, half the bulb being
above the surface of the soil. Water
carefully, and keep completely dark in a
cool cupboard or cellar, or wrapped in a
black plastic bag, at minimum 9° C.
(48° F.) for 8–10 weeks. When the spike
is 5 cm. (2 in.) long, the pot is moved to
a spot at a minimum 12° C. (54° F.),
while the plastic bag is removed and
replaced by a paper hood. After a further period of 2 weeks the pot is taken
into a position at normal room temperature and the paper hood removed when
the bud emerges. During the entire
forcing period meticulous care must
be taken with watering, and the soil
should not be allowed to dry out completely at any time. Normally, 3 months
should be allowed from potting to
flowering.
Suggestion for forcing in bulb glasses:
The glass is filled with water so that the
lower part of the bulb just fails to touch
the surface. The nose is covered with a
paper hood, and the glass placed in a

dark, cool spot at minimum 9° C. (48° F.), for 10 weeks. Look at the glass at least once a week, and top up the water if necessary. When the glass is filled with roots and the spike is 5 cm. (2 in.) long, place the glass in a position at minimum 12° C. (54° F.) for 2 weeks, and after this at normal room temperature. Normally, allow 3 months from putting the bulb in the glass to flowering.

Re-potting: The bulb, once forced, cannot be forced a second time, but may be put out of doors in a garden, where it will produce a fair number of flowers during subsequent years.

Propagation: By side bulbs. Must be entrusted to a bulb specialist.

Varieties: Light red: 'Pink Pearl' and 'Anne Marie'. Sky blue: 'Bismarck'. Medium blue: 'Grand Maître'. White: 'L'Innocence' and 'Queen of the Whites'. The yellow variety 'Yellow Hammer' is not suitable for forcing.

Lilium hybridum (24)

Lily

Habitat: Southern Europe, Eastern Asia and North America.

Growth: Stems 50–100 cm. (2–6 ft.) high, varying according to the different species. The leaves are narrow and shaped like arrows. The flowers are shaped like turbans, trumpets or funnels, upright in some cases and hanging in others. The colours vary from pure white through yellow to orange and red, with an infinite range of nuances. Most of them have a very strong fragrance.

Use: Prepared bulbs for *Lilium auratum* (illustrated).

Lilium longiflorum and *Lilium regale* are forced in commercial nurseries, but further forcing in outdoor culture is complicated and difficult. Pots of forced bulbs which have been purchased can, on the other hand, be used for decoration in rooms and winter gardens.

NOTE: Prepared bulbs have been sub-

jected to various lengths of time at co trolled temperatures, so that they w remain dormant until brought out store and planted. In this way they ca be got to flower at any season.

Soil: Deep pots with rich soil, mix with sand, and good drainage provid by crocks, charcoal and gravel. guard against rotting the bulb its should be bedded on gravel, and shou be covered with a layer of soil as thi as its own height.

Feeding: During the short time spe indoors, feeding is unnecessary.

Water: Plentiful from the reception the bulb until shortly after it has finish flowering. After this, completely dry.

Light: Plenty of daylight, so that stems remain erect.

Heat: The room temperature should be too high.

Air: In very dry room air, gentle spri ling is recommended during the forc period. Otherwise, dry air.

Storage: The bulb is taken from the p and stored for the rest of the winter peat litter—which should be sligh damp—or in sand in a cool cellar.

Planting out: The bulb can be plan out in the spring in a garden and it flower here over a number of ye Forcing for a second time, however, seldom be successful.

Species and varieties: In recent year large number of hybrids have b produced by crossing the many kno species with worthwhile characterist such as strong stems, attractive colo and durable flowers. The Graaf hyb can be recommended in particular.

Sansevieria trifasciata (

Mother-in-law's Tongue

Habitat: Tropical Africa.

Growth: Tough, bayonet-like dark gr leaves, often with attractive pattern grey-green, silvery green and yell Older plants develop upright flo clusters with small greenish-w

owers. The plant often grows to a
etre (3 ft.) in height with good care.
se: Excellent indoor plant, which will
and drought and heat, and which often
rvives for very long periods without
gular attention.
oil: Soilless mixture or ordinary gar-
n soil.
eding: 3 grams per litre (1 oz. per
llon) every week (March–September).
ater: Summer, normal; winter, very
y. Prefers dry soil ball to standing
ter in a base dish.
ght: Full sunlight or other very light
uation. Also survives very well in
rker rooms, but will not then acquire
e attractive patterns on the leaves.
at: High room temperature does no
rm. Winter, not below minimum
°C. (50°F.).
r: Thrives, even in the driest room air.
-potting: February, in pans, so that
roots cannot go too deep.
opagation: By division of root shoots,
ssibly by leaf-cuttings inserted into
ghtly damp sand.
seases: None.
rieties: 'Laurentii', with yellow leaf
ges, and 'Bartels Sensation', which is
y 35 cm. (15 in.) high and has white
f edges.

lipa gesneriana   (26)

lip

bitat: Western Asia.
owth: Fleshy, annual bulb, covered
h a dry tunic. Leaves have no stems
have arched veins. The flowers have
calyces but 6 coloured perianth
ves.
e: Among the many different types,
y the earliest ones are suitable for
cing in a room, whereas none of the
er garden tulips will be successful in
oor culture.
l: Light garden soil mixed with sand.
ding: Unnecessary during forcing,
e the bulb contains all the nourish-
t necessary for flowering.

Water: Pot soil must never be allowed
to dry out, before or during forcing.
Light: Up to the appearance of the buds
the plant must stand in the dark. During
flowering, plenty of light.
Heat: Cool 'preliminary culture' in a
frame in the garden, or in a cellar or
similar location. Forced best at minimum 15°C. (60°F.). When the first
leaves unfold, the temperature is raised
to minimum 20°C. (70°F.). In order to
prolong the flowering period, the plant
may again be placed in a cooler position, e.g. between double windows, when
the flower has fully emerged.
Air: Moist air most suitable. Forced
bulbs must never be brought into dry air
or be left above a radiator.
Suggestion for forcing: Put the bulbs in
pots or flat boxes and place them in a
dark cellar at temperatures as low as
possible. Ten weeks later root formation
is in full swing and the forcing can begin
in a dark room at minimum 15°C.
(60°F.). When the first leaves have
unfolded, put the plant in the light and
raise the temperature to minimum
20°C. (70°F.), until flowering begins.
The best temperature during the actual
flowering period is minimum 16–18°C.
(60–65°F.). Bulbs left in a cellar at
8°C. (48°F.) on 15th September can be
forced at minimum 15°C. (58°F.) from
1st December and at minimum 20°C.
(70°F.) from 1st January. They will
then flower on about 1st February.
Bulbs which have been forced once cannot be forced a second time, but after
flowering has ceased they can be stored
in a dry cool place and planted out in a
garden in April.
Types suitable for forcing: Red:
'Brilliant Star' (particularly early and
very low, so-called 'Christmas tulip'),
'Couleur cardinal', 'Prins van
Oosterrijk' and 'Goya' (abundant
flowering). Yellow: 'Joffre' (particularly
early), 'Bellona' and 'Wilhelm Kordes'
(abundant flowering). White: 'Witte
Valk' and 'Schoonoord' (abundant

Veltheimia capensis

flowering). Two colours: Bi-coloured: 'Keizerskroon' (red and yellow) and 'Pink Beauty' (pink and white).
Other species: See below.

Tulipa praestans 'Fusilier'   (27)

Growth: Dwarf tulip species, which is of interest in that it has many flowers on each stem. Bright red.
Use and culture: As for *Tulipa gesneriana.*

Veltheimia capensis

Habitat: South Africa.
Growth: Bulbous plant with long undulant, dark green leaves. The flower stems are 30–40 cm. (12–16 in.) high and reddish brown. The tube-like, matt, light-red flowers are gathered into a dense cluster.
Use: Durable and ideal indoor plant with long flowering period in winter. Resting period in summer.
Soil: Soilless mixture.
Feeding: 2 grams per litre ($\frac{3}{4}$ oz. per gallon) every 2 weeks (November–February).
Water: Normal, not too lavish from September to June. Should be kept com-

pletely dry during resting period from July to August.
Light: Sunny location in a window facing south. In half-shade there will be more colour on the flowers.
Heat: Winter, minimum 12–20° (54–68° F.); summer, normal temperature. May possibly be left to spend the summer in a warm, sunny place in the garden.
Air: Will stand dry room air.
Re-potting: The best time for re-potting in a slightly larger pot is when the leaf spike breaks through in September after the resting period has ceased. Shake off old earth, and remove dead roots. When planting, one-third of the bulb should be above the surface of the soil.
Propagation: By offshoots, which flower after developing for 3 years.

Yucca aloifolia

Habitat: Central America.
Growth: Slender stems, a metre (3 ft.) in height, with stiff, blue-green leaves provided with a prickly tip. Plants can not flower until they are 10 years old. Large clusters with a great many bell-shaped, white, sweet-scented flowers from July to September.
Use: Space-consuming tub plant,

Yucca aloifolia

rge-scale requirements. Suitable for
nservatories, verandas and patios or
arm terraces during summer.
il: Heavy loam, with good drainage.
eding: 3 grams per litre (1 oz. per
llon) every week (April–September).
ater: Summer, plentiful watering, with
ying out between each occasion; win-
-, dry.
ght: As light as possible.
eat: Summer, normal outdoor tem-
rature. Spring and autumn, minimum
–20° C. (58–70° F.). Winter, only
C. (45° F.) in a light, unheated but
st-free room.
r: Not sensitive to too dry air.
-potting: At intervals of several years.
opagation: By cutting of root shoots,
erwise by seed.
TE: Avoid too much water.
her species: See below

cca recurvifolia

owth: Type with plentiful spread of
nches and yellow-striped leaves.
e and culture: Otherwise the same as
above species.

omeliaceae

chmea fasciata   (28)

bitat: Primeval tropical forests in
tral and South America.
owth: Leaf rosette 50 cm. high and
cm. (20 in.) wide. Like the majority
lants of the pineapple family it is an
hyte, which in its natural environ-
t does not grow with its roots in the
h but on tree branches. Nourishment
water are taken through the upper
s of the leaves, and the leaf rosette
es rainwater for long periods. The
ts do not develop extensively. The
, stiff leaves have toothed edges and
dark green with silvery-grey cross
es. The small blue flowers are short-
d, but are surrounded by stiff, deep
bracts which last for several
ths. The inflorescences rest upon a

Yucca recurvifolia

stiff stem, which sprouts from the middle of the leaf rosette. Only when it is 3
years old is the leaf rosette capable of
flowering, and some time after flowering
the rosette withers away. New inflorescences come from the side shoots at the
base of the old plant.
Use: Good indoor plant, even in warm,
dry rooms. After flowering has ceased, it
is a decorative foliage plant.
Soil: Light soil, rich in humus (leaf
mould, peat or soilless mixture).
Feeding: During the growth period in
spring and summer, minute quantities of
liquid fertiliser should be added to the
soil at 3 weekly intervals, but *never* to
the water in the leaf rosette.
Water: The soil is to be kept slightly
damp, but the water itself must be
administered to the leaf rosette, which
should always contain moisture. Use
rainwater or some other calcium-free
water.
Light: As much as possible, but not in
direct sunshine. Best in windows facing
east, south-east, south-west and west.
Heat: Almost impossible to give it too
much heat. Thrives best at a minimum
25° C. (75° F.). Minimum temperature
in winter 12° C. (55° F.). At a winter
temperature of below 12° C. (55° F.),
growth ceases, the leaves acquire dark
spots and the rosette rots.
Air: Make sure that there is plenty of
fresh air in the summer. Air humidity is
increased by frequent spraying.

Re-potting: Seldom necessary.
Propagation: Side shoots can be taken from older plants and put into new pots in June–July after the main rosette has ceased flowering.
Pests: Occasionally, scale insect and thrips.
NOTE: Always remember the water in the rosette.
Other species: See below.

Aechmea fulgens

Growth: Broad, semi-rigid leaf rosette. Plain, dark green leaves with reddish tinge. Blue flowers surrounded by red bracts.
Use and culture: As for *Aechmea fasciata.*

Billbergia nutans

Habitat: Mexico and South America.
Growth: Like the ordinary pineapple, a terrestial bromeliad with well-developed roots. Better suited to culture in pots than the epiphytic types. Over a period of years, produces thick tufts almost grass-like in character, 50 cm. (20 in.) high. The leaves are narrow, grooved and leathery, with sharp edges. The flowers are gathered into clusters at the tips of the nodding flower stems. The flowers are yellowy-green with blue edges, the surrounding bracts pink. The flower stalks emerge from the middle of the leaf rosette and the rosette dies after flowering has ceased. On the other hand, a number of side shoots develop, which may be left for a number of years in the same flower-pots.
Use: Easy, undemanding room plant which takes well to being left out of doors during the summer. Large plants can be cultivated in large pots or tubs in conservatories.
Soil: Loose soil, rich in humus, e.g. a mixture of leaf mould, peat and sand, possibly soilless mixture.

Feeding: Apply liquid fertiliser sparin[g]ly after flowering has ceased.
Water: Administer direct into the p[ot] Summer, plentiful; winter, more mod[er]ate, depending on temperature.
Light: Light spot not in direct sunligh[t]
Heat: Thrives best at minimum 16° (60° F.) the whole year round. W[ill] however, stand higher temperatures d[ur]ing winter, but not below minim[um] 12° C. (55 F.).
Air: Will stand dry, centrally heated a[ir] but no draughts.
Re-potting: June–July. Water sparin[g] until the new roots have developed.
Propagation: By division of the lar[ge] plants on re-potting.
Pests: Scale insect.
NOTE: Along with *Sansevieria,* one [of] our best indoor plants in dry air.
Other species: See below.

[NOTE: In Great Britain *B. nut[ans]* and *B. windii* are grown at somew[hat] lower temperatures than in Denma[rk] while the other species would be gi[ven] higher temperatures.]

Billbergia fasciata

Growth: The tongue-shaped, bron[ze] green leaves, with yellowish marki[ngs] and prickly edges are gathered int[o a] 40-cm. (1-ft. 3$\frac{1}{4}$-in.)-long tube. The b[lue] flowers with bright red bracts [are] gathered into a nodding inflorescence[.]
Use and culture: As for *Billber[gia] nutans.*

Billbergia vittata

Growth: The tongue-shaped leaves, w[ith] white cross bands on the outer side [and] red spines, are gathered into a me[tre-] long (3-ft.) tube. The leaf tips are ro[lled] back, and the indigo blue flowers w[ith] pink bracts are gathered into a nodd[ing] inflorescence.
Use and culture: As for *Billber[gia] nutans.*

Cryptanthus zonatus zebrinus

ing period during winter, approximately 15° C. (60° F.).

Air: High degree of air humidity.

Other species: See below.

Cryptanthus bivittatus minor

Growth: Olive-green leaves with two pale, salmon-pink longitudinal stripes. In strong light or in soil which is too heavy the colour turns copper-red.

Use and culture: As for *Cryptanthus zonatus.*

Cryptanthus bromelioides tricolor

Growth: Fresh green leaves with ivory-white stripes and pink edges and base. Like a very small *Dracaena.*

Use and culture: As for *Cryptanthus zonatus.*

Billbergia windii (29)

Growth: Vigorous *Billbergia* type. The flowers proper are long, pointed and yellowy-green. The bracts are very large and broad, and deep pink in colour.

Use and culture: As for *Billbergia* ...ans.

Cryptanthus zonatus zebrinus

Habitat: Tropical forest ground plant in Brazil (individual species live as epiphytes or more often as lithophytes on rocks).

Growth: Flat leaf rosette up to 15 cm. (6 in.) across and seldom more than 3 cm. (just over an inch) high. The stiff, leathery, undulant leaves are an elegant bronze-purple colour, with silvery-grey cross bands. The flowers are small and unattractive.

Use: Decorative, but not a particularly durable indoor plant. As a rule grows well only for short periods, best in a conservatory or greenhouse.

...: Developed best as an epiphyte, grown on a piece of bark. May also do well hanging on a piece of steel wire in a window, without any kind of root support. Treated in pots with very light soil (peat or loamless compost).

...ding: Not necessary.

...er: Only in the leaf rosette.

...t: Requires a lot of light, but never direct sunlight.

...t: Summer, even high temperature, approximately 25° C. (80° F.); in rest-

Guzmania monostachya

Habitat: Tropical rain forests in Central and South America.

Growth: Epiphyte with 50-cm. (20-in.) high, funnel-shaped leaf rosette. The leaves are fully rounded at the edges and are greenish in colour. The round flower stems are covered with small red bracts with white tips. Flowers and floral bracts have black, white and red colours. The flowers last for about 14 days.

Guzmania monostachya

Use: Best in conservatories or in hothouses.
Culture: As for *Aechmea fasciata.*
Other species: See below.

Guzmania minor

Growth: 20-cm. (8-in.)-high leaf rosette. The leaves are reddish-orange. The flowers are white with red bracts. More durable than *Guzmania monostachya.* Use and culture are otherwise the same as for this type.

Neoregelia carolinae

Habitat: Tropical rain forests in Brazil.
Growth: Epiphyte with dense, flat rosette with broad leaf sheathes around the stemless, pincushion-like inflorescences. The leaves are tongue-shaped and coriaceous, with fine prickles around the edges. Both sides are green, but the innermost leaves turn blood-red when flowering takes place. The red colouring lasts for several months. The flowers are very small and reddish-violet.
Use: Best in conservatories and greenhouses.
Culture: As for *Aechmea fasciata,* but requires consistently high temperatures and high degree of air humidity all the year round.
NOTE: Limited durability. The variety *tricolor,* with leaves variegated with longitudinal yellow and cream stripes, is the form most commonly met.

Nidularium innocentii   (30)

Habitat: Brazil. The Latin name, which means 'little bird's nest', refers to the inflorescences, which are right in the middle of the leaf rosettes.
Growth: As for *Neoregelia carolinae,* from which it may be difficult to distinguish. The leaves are broadest at the bottom and have toothed edges; their upper side is dark green, the underside

blackish-green. The central lea▸ remain bright copper red during ▮ whole of the flowering period. T▮ inconspicuous white flowers are hidd▸ in the 'bird's nest'.
Use: Best in a hothouse.
Culture: As for *Aechmea fasciata,* ▮ requires constant high temperatu▸ ample degree of air humidity a▮ shade.
NOTE: Limited durability indoors.
Other species: See below.

Nidularium fulgens

Growth: Leaves are pale green with d▸ green spots and serrated edges. The c▸ tral leaves are scarlet, the flowers vi◂ with white tubes.
Use and culture: As for *Nidulari▸ innocentii.*

Tillandsia cyanea   (

Habitat: Ecuador.
Growth: Elegant leaf rosette, wh▸ readily develops side shoots. The lea▸ are dark green, narrow and sharp-edg▸ The 20-cm. (8-in.)-high flower stem e▸ at the top in a flat diamond-shaped, l▸ red spike, and the large indivi◂ flowers emerge between the bract▸ this, one at a time. They are an int▸ blue in colour, and although eac▮ short-lived the complete flowe▸ extends over a long period.
Use: Good and durable indoor plant▸
Culture: As for *Aechmea fasciata.*
Other species: See below.

Tillandsia lindenii

Growth: Larger than *Tillandsia cya▸ up to 50 cm. (20 in.) in height. Use ▸ culture otherwise as for this species.

Vriesia hieroglyphica

Habitat: Tropical rain forests in Ce▸ and South America.
Growth: Leaf rosette up to 50

Vriesia hieroglyphica

in.) in height, and of equal width; h leaf 6–8 cm. (2–3 in.) broad, with a rp tip. The colour is grey-green, with wnish, uneven transverse stripes ch are somewhat reminiscent of dwritten characters, hence the name. tivated for the sake of the attractive es. The flowers are spread out on a cm. (20-in.) high stem, and the plant only flower after 4 years' growth.

: Durable and well suited to cultiva- in a room or a conservatory.

ture: As for *Aechmea fasciata*. Must protected, especially against direct ight. Only use water which is cal- n free, which should be poured ctly into the leaf rosette. Re potting ecessary.

ases: Yellow leaves are a sign of too ch sunlight.

er species: See below.

sia splendens (32)

wth: Leaves 4–6 cm. (1½–2½ in.) d, vivid green in colour, with brown s stripes. A broad, thick, sword- ed spike protrudes from the leaf te. The flowers are yellow and short-

lived, while the fiery red bracts remain for a long time. May flower at any time.

Use and culture: As for *Vriesia hieroglyphica*, but give more light.

Amaryllidaceae

Agave americana (33)

Century Plant

Habitat: Mexico and Central America.

Growth: Rigid, fleshy leaves, gathered into a decorative rosette. The leaf edges are prickly and the leaf tip has a very sharp spine which may be a danger to anyone in the plant's immediate vicinity. The leaves are blue-green, often with yellow longitudinal stripes or edges. Only the older plants flower, with a 2–5-m. (6½–16-ft.)-high flower stem, after which the plant dies.

Use: Very large tub plant for conserva- tories, suitable for patios and terraces during the summer. The leaf tips are provided with cork stops during trans- port, to avoid accidents. Should not be kept in homes where there are small children.

Soil: Soilless mixture.

Feeding: 3 grams per litre (1 oz. per gallon) every 2 weeks (March– September).

Water: Plenty during the summer, dry in winter.

Light: Light, sunny growth spot, par- ticularly in winter.

Heat: Summer, best out of doors; win- ter, minimum 4–8° C. (40–45° F.). Will not stand frost.

Air: Likes dry air.

Re-potting: Every 3 years in February.

Propagation: By cutting the small rosettes on the runners.

Diseases: Brown spots on leaves from too much warmth, darkness or humidity during winter.

Variant: 'Variegata', with yellow stripes along the edges of the leaves.

NOTE: Take care with the spiny leaf tips.

Other species: See below.

Agave filifera

Growth: No prickly edges, but with a row of bristles along the edges of the leaves.

Use and culture: As for *Agave americana.*

Clivia miniata (34)

Kaffir Lily

Habitat: South Africa.

Growth: Fleshy roots. Thick leaf sheaths with dark green leaves, which branch out alternately on both sides. The 50-cm. (20-in.)-high, flat flower stems bear 10–20 orange-red-coloured flowers in the spring, and occasionally also in the autumn.

Use: Undemanding, perennial indoor plant, which must always be kept in the same place and position. Not even the pot should be turned.

Soil: Soilless mixture, or heavy, somewhat clayey garden soil. pH 7.

Feeding: 3 grams per litre (1 oz. per gallon) every week (March–August).

Water: Will not stand constant moisture. During the growth period from February to August, the pot must be allowed to dry out between each thorough watering. During the resting period from September to January, the plant must be allowed to remain completely dry.

Light: Best in a light window with slight shade.

Heat: Normal room temperature, not below minimum 15° C. (60° F.). When temperatures are too low during the development of flowers, the flower stems will not have the desired length, and the flowers will remain down in between the leaves. In the resting period in autumn and winter, best at minimum 12° C. (55° F.).

Air: Will stand dry room air, but likes syringing during growth period *after* flowering has ceased.

Re-potting: After flowering has ceased,

Eucharis grandiflora

in spacious pots. Careful watering a re-potting, so that the fleshy roots do rot.

Cutting: The flower stems are cut ou the normal way after flowering ceased.

Propagation: By division after flower has ceased. Second-year plants are g erally capable of flowering.

NOTE: Failure to flower may be due the fact that the resting period has been properly provided for.

Eucharis grandiflora

Habitat: South America.

Growth: The leaves are arum-like. 50-cm. (20-in.)-high, upright flo stems are without leaves. The like, pure white, delicately frag flowers have a perianth with jag edges and green stripes. Continuo flowering so long as growth is not tarded.

Use: Somewhat difficult indoor pl which requires constant humidity a temperature of minimum 20° C. (70 all the year round.

Soil: Deep pots with at least 20 (8 in.) of soil, consisting of strong e mould, with leaf mould and sand m in.

Feeding: 2 grams per litre ($\frac{3}{4}$ oz.

lon) every week (March–October).
orporate plenty of bonemeal in the
ting compost.
ter: Grows in nature in river deltas,
ich is why it needs constant watering
l must never dry out.
ht: Best in a light window, but never
lirect sunlight.
at: Very demanding with regard to
t, not below minimum 20° C.
° F.).
: Humid air with frequent syring-

potting: Every 2 years. The bulb tips
st be flush with the surface of the soil.
pagation: By side bulbs with at least
leaf.
E: Flowers attractive, and durable
n out.

manthus albiflos

itat: South Africa.
wth: Bulbous plant, with a few
green, downy leaves. Flowers are
e with bunches of yellow stamens
gathered into an inflorescence like a
ing brush. Flowers in the spring.
: Durable and rewarding indoor
t, even in centrally heated rooms.
: Soilless mixture.
ding: 2 grams of fertiliser per litre
. per gallon) of water every 2 weeks
y–July). Plants which receive too
h nourishment have difficulty in
ng through the winter.
er: Normal watering in summer;
August to the end of January, very
Will prefer being dried out com
ly to being overwatered.
t: Full sunlight.
: Normal room temperature; in
er best at minimum 12–16° C. (55–
F.).
Dry air.
otting: Every 2 years. Only half of
ulb must be covered with soil.
agation: By division.
species: See below.

Haemanthus katherinae

Growth: Vigorous. The undulant green
leaves wither in the autumn. The large
inflorescence has deep red flowers, with
blood-red stamens and pistils. The
flowering season is during the height of
the summer. The name 'Blood-flower'
relates to the red sap which appears
when the leaves or stems are lacerated.
Use and culture: As for *Haemanthus
albiflos*, but requires higher temperature
and higher degree of air humidity.

Haemanthus puniceus (35)

Growth: Shorter stems and smaller
flowers than the other *Haemanthus*
species. The flowers are bright red.
Use and culture: As for *Haemanthus
albiflos*, but requires higher degree of air
humidity.

Hippeastrum hortorum (36)

Amaryllis

Habitat: South America.
Growth: Vigorous bulb with fleshy
roots. The leaves are long and ribbon-
like. One or two strong flower stems,
each with 4–6 trumpet-shaped flowers
in white, pale red or dark red.
Use: Easy forcing plant for flowering at
Christmas or after.
Soil: Soilless mixture, with good drainage. Only half of the bulb must be
covered with soil.
Feeding: 5 grams of fertiliser per litre
(1½ oz. per gallon) of water every 2
weeks from the end of flowering to the
beginning of the resting period in
September–October. No feeding during
the flowering season.
Water: Dry during the resting period
and until the flower shoot has emerged.
After that, plentiful watering during the
flowering and growing season in spring
and summer.
Light: Light and sunny situation from

the end of flowering until October. Remember to keep the flower shoot in shade during its development, so as to assist the lengthening of the stem.

Heat: During forcing, minimum 20–25° C. (70–80° F.). Afterwards, cooler. In summer, out of doors on a balcony or in a garden.

Air: Spray during the development of leaves and flowers.

Re-potting: Every 3 or 4 years in larger pots. Only half of the bulbs flower when forced a second time, therefore attempts at this are usually disappointing.

Propagation: By seed or side bulbs.

Suggestion for forcing: Having bought the bulbs, place them in lukewarm water for 24 hours. Then plant them in soilless mixture in plastic pots with at least 2 cm. ($\frac{3}{4}$ in.) drainage at the bottom. The soil should only cover half the bulb, and should be loose underneath and around it. The bulb should then be covered with a paper hood, and placed in direct heat, possibly near a radiator. Give just enough water to ensure that the soil does not dry out completely. Water more generously when the spike is 10 cm. (4 in.) long, and remove the paper hood. Care with watering and feeding after flowering is important if there is to be the possibility of forcing and flowering again the following year. The resting period, October–December, must not be neglected; during this time the leaves die and the old roots dry up, and the plant must be kept cool, protected from frost and absolutely dry.

NOTE: You can only depend on flowering if you force new bulbs each year. A better result is obtained with *Vallota speciosa*, which see.

Hymenocallis speciosa

Habitat: West Indies.

Growth: Vigorous bulb plant with broad, ribbon-like leaves. The white flowers, which have a vanilla fragrance, are gathered 10–12 together into an

Hymenocallis speciosa

umbel, the outer ones opening out f Flowering may take place at any t during the year, though normally in autumn.

Use: Hothouse plant, which require high soil and air temperature the w year round. No real resting period. suited for warm conservatory or gr house.

Soil: Soilless mixture (in large pots).

Feeding: 3 grams of fertiliser per lit water (1 oz. per gallon) each week ing the summer.

Water: Summer, frequent wate During the winter use only water the chill taken off it. The soil must be cooled by cold water.

Light: Plenty, but no direct sunlight

Heat: Best at minimum 20° C. (70 the whole year round.

Air: Summer, humid air; winter, dri

Re-potting: After flowering has ce Avoid lacerating or drying out roots.

Propagation: By side bulbs.

Other species: See below.

Hymenocallis macrostephana

Habitat: Bolivia.

Growth: Flowers in the summer.

e and culture: As for *Hymenocallis*
·ciosa, but does not require quite such
.h temperatures. Resting period from
otember to March, during which the
b should be kept dry and cool at a
nimum 10° C. (50° F.).

rcissus pseudonarcissus   (37)

ffodil

bitat: Western Europe.

wth: Vigorous, perennial bulb with
row linear leaves. Only one flower on
h stem. The flower has a protruding,
ar-like perianth and a trumpet-
ped corona.

: As easy to force as *Hyacinthus*
ntalis, but best at relatively low tem-
ature.

l: Ordinary garden soil mixed with
d.

ding: Unnecessary before and during
ing, since the bulb contains the
ients necessary for flowering.

er: The soil must never dry out;
rous watering is thus required.

it: The spike must be protected from
daylight by a paper hood, as for
inth forcing.

t: During the development of roots,
mum 5° C. (40° F.), afterwards
mum 10° C. (50° F.). When the
er buds appear, at minimum 15° C.
F.), and when they open out, ordin-
oom temperature.

Thrives in dry centrally heated air,
ikes syringing during forcing.

otting: The bulbs cannot be forced a
cond time, but can be used in the
en. The forced bulbs must be put
of doors as soon as they can be got
the soil.

agation: By side bulbs.

estion for forcing in pots:
rence should be given to large
le-nosed' bulbs, since each 'nose'
uces one flower. They are placed in
pots in August–September, and
in a cool cellar at a minimum 5° C.
F.) for 6 weeks; afterwards at a

minimum 10° C. (50° F.) for 4 weeks;
for a time at a minimum 15° C. (60° F.),
until the flower stems grow longer; finally, at normal room temperature. In
order to obtain sufficiently long stems,
the paper hood is not removed until the
bud is beginning to emerge. The bulbs
must be inspected regularly to ensure
that the soil never dries out. After
flowering, the bulbs are placed in a light,
cool place, but are kept regularly
watered, until they can be planted out in
the garden in April.

Forcing in a bulb jar: Like hyacinths,
the bulbs can also be forced in a bulb
jar, but unlike them, they must not come
into contact with the water. The heavy
top part must be supported so that it
does not overturn.

Forcing in artificial light: Narcissus
bulbs may be forced with 12 hours' daylight. The plant's natural flowering takes
place at the spring equinox, when it is
affected by the regular alternation between 12 hours of daylight and 12 hours
of darkness. The bulbs should be
planted as usual in pots or boxes and
kept in earth pits or cellars at low temperatures. When the spikes are 5 cm.
(2 in.) long late in November the bulbs
are placed in a cellar, where, with the aid
of lamp bulbs or fluorescent tubes, they
are given 12 hours' light alternated with
12 hours' darkness. The lamps should
give off 1,000 watts per square yard of
floor area, and be suspended at 100 cm.
(3 ft.) above the plants. Air temperature
should be a minimum 18° C. (65° F.).
When the buds begin to colour, the
bulbs are taken into the house.

Types suitable for forcing: 'Golden
Harvest' and 'King Alfred'.

Other species: See below.

Narcissus tazetta totus albus

Paper-white Narcissus

Growth: A large number of small, star-
shaped flowers on each stem. Delicate
fragrance.

Narcissus totus albus

Forcing: The bulbs are planted in dishes with gravel or pebbles, at normal room temperatures for 7 weeks without pre-culture, in a cool, dark atmosphere. There should be standing water in the dish the whole time, up to the middle of the bulb. The bulbs are discarded after flowering once, and cannot be used in the garden since they are not sufficiently hardy for our climate.

Narcissus poetaz (38)

Growth: Several small, cup-shaped flowers with a little, flat corona on each stem. Delicate fragrance.

Varieties suitable for forcing: Abundant flowering: 'Cheerfulness' (cream coloured). Single flowers: 'Scarlet Gem' (pale yellow and orange-yellow) and 'Geranium' (white and orange-yellow). These varieties can be forced as indicated for *Narcissus pseudo-narcissus*. 'Cragford' (white and orange) may be forced in dishes with pebbles and water, like *Narcissus totus albus*.

Sprekelia formosissima (39)

Jacobean Lily

Habitat: Mexico.
Growth: Dark bulbs, narrow ribbon-like leaves and an unusual, cross-shap velvet-red flower, the shape of which reminiscent of the cross of the Span Crusaders' patron saint, Saint James Calatrava.

Use: Summer-flowering bulb plant rooms, winter gardens or warm su spots out of doors. Should be plante early spring, flowers in May–June, is taken up in the autumn for warm dry wintering.

Soil: Soilless mixture.

Feeding: 3 grams of fertiliser per (1 oz. per gallon) of water every w May–July.

Water: After planting, water caref but more copiously when the le appear. Watering should be stop when the leaves wither in August, the plant should be kept completely for the rest of the year.

Light: Sunlight.

Heat: Summer, normal temperat winter, minimum 12° C. (55° F.). If too cool during the winter, it will flower the following summer.

Air: Normal, dry indoor air.

Re-potting: January–February, be growth gets under way.

Propagation: By side bulbs. Seed flower when 4 years old.

Vallota speciosa

Scarborough Lily

Habitat: South Africa.

Growth: Reminiscent of *Amaryllis* less vigorous and flowers in Aug September. The bulb is brown, leaves and stems 30 cm. (12 in.) the flowers bright red.

Use: Very attractive and good, summer flowering indoor plant. E flowers a second time. Resents disturbances and thrives in the sam for many years.

Soil: Soilless mixture.

Feeding: 3 grams of fertiliser per li oz. per gallon) of water every 2 v (March–August).

ater: Normal watering during the
...ole of the growth period until flower-
...g. Afterwards, only small amounts,
...d completely dry in winter. Very
...ung plants should, however, have
...ghtly moist soil balls even in win-
...

...ht: Likes full sunlight.
...at: Normal room temperature. Older,
...wering plants should spend the winter
... minimum 12° C. (55° F.), young
...nts at minimum 15–20° C. (60–
...° F.) so that they can continue their
...wth without a period of rest.
...: Will stand dry room air.
...potting: Early spring in pots which
... not too large. The fleshy roots must
...handled with care, so that they do not
...p or become damaged.
...pagation: By side bulbs, which will
...ver after 3 years' development.
...TE: An easy, summer-flowering bulb
...nt which may be recommended.

...phyranthes grandiflora

...bitat: Central America.
...wth: Small, short-necked, oval bulb
... 20-cm. (8-in.) linear leaves. The
...us bear one erect, funnel-shaped
...er, which is luminous pink in
...ur.
...: Attractive spring- and summer-
...ering bulb plant for rooms and con-

Zephyranthes grandiflora

servatories. When not in flower, the
plant has no attraction.
Soil: Soilless mixture.
Feeding: 2 grams of fertiliser per litre
($\frac{1}{4}$ oz. per gallon) of water every 2 weeks
in summer.
Water: Summer, plentiful; winter, more
sparingly, but without allowing the soil
to dry out completely.
Light: Sunny spot.
Heat: Normal room temperature; winter, now below minimum 10° C.
(50° F.). Will not stand frost at all.
Air: Will stand dry room air.
Re-potting: Spring, before growth
begins.
Propagation: Develops a number of side
bulbs.

Orchidaceae

Orchids

Habitat: The orchid family covers a
large number of genera, from a wide
variety of climatic conditions, with
varying temperature, air humidity and
soil requirements.
Growth: Many orchids are epiphytes.
When growing wild, their roots suck in
nourishment from rotten plant fragments and moss on tree bark. Others
grow with their roots directly in the
earth, often in symbiosis with certain
types of fungus.
Use: Most orchids are only suitable
for cultivation in specially arranged
greenhouses or flower windows. Few
can be used for normal indoor culture.
A very few are fragrant. Orchids have
a number of cultural requirements in
common, which are described immediately below, while the special requirements are indicated for the individual
types.
Soil: Orchid soil is a mixture consisting
of fern fibres (from Osmunda- or tree-
ferns), peat, sphagnum moss, beech
leaves and bark. The nutrients in this
light soil are converted more rapidly

than those in ordinary soil, which is why orchids must be frequently re-potted, and the intervals between re-potting depend on the consistency of the soil mixture. In the U.S.A. the epiphytic species are more commonly potted in chunks of fir bark, sold under various trade names.

Other common culture requirements: Rainwater or some other soft water must be used for watering. Nourishment requirements are more modest than for other indoor plants (half quantities). Temperature requirements vary for the different kinds and must be adhered to rigidly. If the resting period is not observed, flowering will fail.

Genera and species: See below.

Cattleya labiata (41)

Cattleya

Habitat: Central and South America.

Growth: Creeping rhizome with thick pseudo-bulbs, each with one or two coriaceous, evergreen leaves. The inflorescence emerges from the latest developed pseudo-bulb and has one or more flowers. Every flower has 3 sepals and 3 petals, of which one—the lip—is the largest and has the deepest colour. Many colours are represented: white, yellow, pink, mauve, violet and red. Flowering begins a few months after the bulb has reached full growth; after flowering, there is a resting period of 4 weeks, during which no water should be given.

Use: Hybrids are more suitable for indoor culture.

Soil: Compost, consisting of fern fibre, sphagnum and beech leaves.

Feeding: 1 gram of fertiliser per litre ($\frac{1}{4}$ oz. per gallon) of water every 2 weeks during the growth period. (Most orchid growers never use fertiliser except as a foliar feed.)

Water: Water generously during the summer, while the soil should be

Coelogyne cristata

allowed to dry out between each watering during the winter. No water during the resting period.

Light: Requires as much light as possible. Flower-pots or plant-boxes must, however, be protected against direct sunlight.

Heat: Minimum 20° C. (70° F.) during the day, somewhat cooler at night. Minimum temperature in winter 14° (57° F.).

Air: Will stand dry room air very well. Frequent syringing during hot weather.

Re-potting: After flowering, when compost has decayed and is loose. Take care that the plant is bedded in firmly.

Propagation: By division. With every pseudo-bulb which is separated from the parent plant, a latent bud should develop.

NOTE: Concerning culture requirements in general, see *Orchids*.

Coelogyne cristata

Habitat: Ceylon, East Indies, Samoa.

Growth: Fleshy, slightly wrinkled pseudo-bulbs, pointed leaves and hanging inflorescences with white, yellow edged flowers, October—November.

Use: Easy indoor orchid, which must be kept during the summer in a slightly shaded place in the garden, and possibly suspended in the crown of a tree.

il: Cultivated in a box or pot with
mpost, consisting of sphagnum,
redded bark and beech leaves

eding: 1 gram of fertiliser per litre
oz. per gallon) of water every 3 weeks
ring the growth period.

ater: Water generously in summer;
er flowering, relatively dry.

ght: Slight shade in a window facing
st, west or north.

at: Minimum 15–20° C. (60–70° F.)

r: Likes humid air, best in living-
oms or kitchens with a high degree of
humidity. Frequent sprinkling, espe-
lly during hot weather.

potting: As for *Cattleya labiata.*
lture requirements in general, see
chids.

mbidium pumilum (42)

bitat: China and Japan.

owth: Epiphyte, with a short rhizome
ich has a large number of small, long-
ing white, yellow and brown flowers
he winter.

cial culture requirements: Good
oor orchid under cool conditions—a
ter temperature of 10° C. (50° F.)
summer temperature not exceeding
C. (70° F.). Cultivated in orchid soil
plastic pots with good drainage.
ge amounts of light and water during
growth period. A resting period of 4
ks in the autumn is necessary for
ering. Concerning culture require-
ts in general, see *Orchids.*

e: A very tricky indoor plant for
teurs.

hiopedilum (Cypripedium) hy-
lum (43)

per Orchid

itat: Tropical Asia.

wth: Winter-flowering terrestial
id without pseudo-bulbs. Decora-
leaves, often with attractive mark-
in dark green and brown. The
ers, which are borne singly on rigid

stems and are very durable, have a waxy
appearance with dark, shoe-shaped lips
and lighter perianths with attractive patterns in white, yellow, green and brown.
Innumerable varieties.

Use: Easy indoor orchid for flower pots,
preferably plastic pots with good drainage. The green-leafed varieties are best
in cool locations. Those with mottled
leaves do well in normal room temperatures. A 5-week resting period,
September–October, is necessary for
flowering in January–February.

Soil: Sphagnum, with shredded bark
and beech leaves added.

Feeding: 1 gram of fertiliser per litre
($\frac{1}{4}$ oz. per gallon) of water every 2 weeks
during the growth period.

Water: Ordinary tap water (not rainwater). Give even watering the whole
year round and never allow to become
bone-dry. Should only be dry during
resting period and immediately after re-
potting.

Light: Slight shade.

Heat: Normal room temperature, but
only minimum 10–12° C. (50–55° F.)
during resting period.

Air: Spray during hot periods.

Repotting: After flowering has ceased,
late winter. Firm potting. No water for
14 days afterwards.

NOTE: If the resting period is not
observed, flowering will fail, which
applies to all the *Paphiopedilum* types.

Other species: See below.

Dendrobium nobile

Habitat: Southern Asia and Australia.

Growth: Epiphyte with long, thin
pseudobulbs, each with 2–3 flowers in
pink, violet and white in early spring.
The roots spread themselves out on the
surface of the soil.

Use: Rewarding indoor plant which
flowers annually.

Soil: Cultivated in a very small pot with
just a little orchid soil. The bottom two-
thirds of the pot are filled with broken

Dendrobium nobile

crocks for drainage, so as to avoid constant moisture. An orchid basket is also suitable for cultivation.

Feeding: 1 gram fertiliser per litre of water ($\frac{1}{4}$ oz. per gallon) every 3 weeks during the growth period.

Water: Frequent watering, since the compost quickly dries out with the efficient drainage arrangement used. New shoots will rot with excessive moisture. When the bulbs have developed sufficiently the plant must be kept completely dry during the winter, until the flower buds are just developing.

Light: Plenty of light.

Heat: Very warm during the summer, winter cool (minimum 6–15° C. or 45–60° F.). A high winter temperature coupled with dampness produces a number of small plants instead of flower buds.

Air: Frequent sprinkling in hot weather.

Re-potting: After flowering has ceased.

Concerning culture requirements in general, see *Orchids*.

Other species: See below.

Dendrobium phalaenopsis

Growth: Large stems with 10–20 long-lasting flowers in autumn and winter. Pink, dark purple and white varieties.

Culture requirements: As f Dendrobium nobile, but to be cultivat in warmth the whole year round.

NOTE: Very difficult plant for amateur

Epidendrum vitellinum

Habitat: Mountainous regions Mexico.

Growth: Compact plant with sho thick pseudo-bulbs, having dura orange-red flowers measuring 5 c (nearly 2 in.) in great profusion 20-cm. (8-in.)-high stems.

Special culture requirements: Fares b at steady, cool room temperatures a in large amounts of light. No defir resting period. Concerning cultu requirements in general, see *Orchids*.

Odontoglossum grande (

Habitat: Cool mountainous regions Tropical America.

Growth: Winter-flowering plant with 5 very large, yellow flowers with bro blotches and stripes.

Special culture requirements: E indoor orchid under cool conditi (minimum 15° C. or 60° F.) and he shade, e.g. in a light window fac north. Can be left to spend the sum

Epidendrum vitellinum

a garden. Concerning culture require-
ents in general, see *Orchids*.
ther species: See below.

dontoglossum pulchellum

rowth: Shining pure white flowers with
ellow spots on the lips. It is very frag-
nt.
ulture: As for *Odontoglossum grande*.

ncidium ornithorhynchum   (45)

abitat: Tropical America.
owth: Epiphyte with thick pseudo-
lbs and flower stems 30 cm. (12 in.)
ng, bearing a very large number of
all mauve flowers in autumn and win-
. Delicate fragrance.
ecial culture requirements: Cultivated
a block of bark or in a basket, so as
avoid constant dampness at the roots.
ghtly shaded situation in a room
ich is not too warm (minimum 15°C.
60°F.). Concerning culture require-
nts in general, see *Orchids*.

phiopedilum callosum

owth: Marbled leaves and white-
en flowers with brownish-violet
pes.
e and culture: As for *Paphiopedilum
bridum*, but best at minimum 18°C.
°F.).

phiopedilum insigne

owth: Green leaves. Flowers white or
e green with brown markings.
e and culture: As for *Paphiopedilum
ridum*, but requires somewhat lower
mperature (minimum 14°C. or
°F.).

phiopedilum villosum

owth: Light brown flowers. Vigorous
wth.

Calathea insignis

Use and culture: As for *Paphiopedilum
hybridum*, but best at minimum 16°C.
(60°F.).

Marantaceae

Calathea insignis

Habitat: Damp forests in Tropical
America.
Growth: Foliage plant with light green
leaves bearing attractive, leaf-shaped
markings in dark green.
Use: Heat-demanding plant. Best in
warm conservatories, or as a short-lived
ornamental plant in warm rooms.
Soil: Soilless mixture with good drain-
age.
Feeding: 3 grams of fertiliser per litre
(1 oz. per gallon) of water every 2 weeks
(March–August).
Water: Never allow to dry out com-
pletely, but must not be too damp, espe-
cially in the winter-time.
Light: Full or half-shade.
Heat: Best at minimum 22–25°C. (70–
80°F.), never below 15°C. (60°F.).
Air: High degree of air humidity, fre-
quent spraying the whole year round.
Re-potting: Spring, in pots which are not
too large.
Propagation: By division.
Pests: Red spider mites.

Maranta leuconeura
kerchoveana (46)

Prayer Plant

Habitat: Tropical America.

Growth: 20-cm. (8-in.)-high foliage plant, with green, oval leaves which have pairs of dark green spots on both sides of the midrib. On young leaves the markings are olive-green or brown. The leaf veins stand out and are silvery-grey, like fishbones. During the evening and night, the leaves turn themselves in pairs into a vertical sleeping position.

Use: Ornamental foliage plant in slightly shaded flower windows or winter gardens.

Soil: Soilless mixture.

Feeding: 1 gram of fertiliser per litre ($\frac{1}{4}$ oz. per gallon) of water every 2 weeks (April–August).

Water: Never allow to dry out completely, as this will cause brown edges on the leaves.

Light: Half-shade, never direct sunlight.

Heat: Requires a lot of heat; winter, not below minimum 18°C. (65°F.).

Air: Will not stand draughts. Best in humid air. Sprinkling with lime-free water during the summer.

Re-potting: February, in pans with ample drainage.

Propagation: By division.

Pests: Slugs and snails, wood lice.

Moraceae

Ficus benjamina (47)

Habitat: The Tropics.

Growth: Loose, pendulous growth, like a birch tree. Small, pointed dark green leaves.

Use: Elegant indoor plant, which, however, under good conditions quickly grows too large for an ordinary window-sill. Well suited for conservatories or as an ornamental plant for larger rooms.

Soil: Soilless mixture (very large pots).

Feeding: 3 grams of fertiliser per lit (1 oz. per gallon) of water every 2 wee (February–September). Never feed du ing winter.

Water: Water generously during t. summer; avoid drying out complete! The pot should be evenly damp duri the winter.

Light: Semi-shaded or light situation. heavy shade the leaves are gradual shed.

Heat: Normal room temperature; w ter, best at minimum 16–20°C. (6 70°F.).

Air: Dry room air.

Re-potting: Early spring.

Propagation: By cuttings, with high b tom heat.

Pests: Red spider mites.

Other species: See below.

Ficus carica (4

Fig

Habitat: Mediterranean countries a the Orient.

Growth: Deciduous tree with attracti pale grey bark, sharply lobed leaves a green or violet pleasant-tasting fruits.

Use: May be cultivated in cool cons vatories, cold greenhouses or out doors in protected locations on so walls, possibly as a tub plant on a race, wintering in a light frost-free ro Small plants are decorative on wind sills. Seldom bears fruit indoors.

Soil: Standard potting mixture or g den soil with peat and sand added.

Feeding: 6 grams of fertiliser per (2 oz. per gallon) of water every 2 we during the growth period.

Water: Water generously in the spr and early summer, after which keep and in winter completely dry.

Light: As light as possible.

Heat: Summer, normal temperat winter, minimum 5°C. (40°F.).

Air: Spraying during growth period.

Re-potting: When the roots fill the po tub.

Ficus diversifolia

tting: Plants which are too big can be back in the late autumn or in winter.
propagation: By seed (or by rooting kers).

us diversifolia

stletoe Fig

bitat: Tropical rain forests in Java.
owth: Bush-like, with oval leaves ich have small black dots on their dersides. The tiny, berry-like, red or ow fruits are found in great profu-.

: Decorative 'fruit plant' in semi-ded windows.
ture: As for *Ficus benjamina.*

us elastica (49)

ia Rubber Plant

bitat: Tropical rain forests in Eastern a.
wth: Vigorous, erect plant, with y, coriaceous, dark green leaves. noving the growing point will cause ching.

Use: Good indoor plant, even in shady rooms. Best in the same location the whole year round.
Culture: As for *Ficus benjamina.* Best winter temperature, however, minimum 15° C. (60° F.).
Pests: Red spider mites in too harsh sunlight, scale insects, mealy bug.
Diseases: The bottom leaves are shed when the plant lacks nourishment. If the winter conditions are too damp the plant is easily destroyed. With too much heat the leaves hang down limply.
Varieties: decora, which has broad, oval leaves and is not very demanding; *schyveriana,* with broad, greenish-yellow marbled leaves, and 'Variegata' with narrow, white or yellow multi-coloured leaves.
NOTE: Clean dusty leaves with soft soapy water (not synthetic detergent), and rinse with plain water, preferably rainwater.

Ficus lyrata

Fiddle-leaf Fig

Habitat: West Africa.
Growth: Large, violin-shaped, shiny leaves.

Ficus lyrata

Ficus radicans

Use: Not so durable in a room, best in a conservatory or a hall.
Culture: As for *Ficus benjamina*. Will not stand draughts or temperatures which are too low.

Ficus pumila (50)
Creeping Fig

Habitat: China, Japan and Australia.
Growth: Climbing plant with small, dense, oval leaves. Without a base or support for the suction roots the plant will take on a hanging growth.
Use: Suitable as a hanging-bowl plant or as creeping ground covering in flower windows or conservatories.
Culture: As for *Ficus benjamina*, but will thrive under much cooler conditions and requires constant shade.
Variant: minima, with leaves which are hardly 1 cm. ($\frac{2}{5}$ in.) long.

Ficus radicans

Growth: More vigorous than *Ficus pumila* with large, pointed leaves and the same creeping growth. Runners up to 5 metres (15 ft.) long under good conditions in a conservatory or hothouse. Used and cultivated otherwise as the species described above.

Ficus religiosa
'Peepul'.

Habitat: East Indies and Ceylon. T Buddhists' holy tree, under which according to tradition—Buddha saw visions. Offshoots are planted in templ all over the East.
Growth: A deciduous tree having mc than one trunk with elegant poplar-li leaves with extended tips.
Use: Suitable for conservatories a greenhouses.
Culture: As for *Ficus benjamina*.

Urticaceae

Helxine soleirolii
'Mind your own business'
Known exclusively in U.S.A. as 'Bab Tears'

Habitat: Corsica.
Growth: Low, creeping, succulent-gr plant with small, rounded leav Quickly covers the pot and hangs do over the sides.
Use: Hanging-bowl plant. Apart fr this, it is suitable as a ground cover

Ficus religiosa

r conservatories, flower windows or
varia.

oil: Soilless mixture.

eeding: 2 grams of fertiliser per litre
 oz. per gallon) of water every 2
eeks, as far as possible without mois-
ning the leaves with the water, which
ay scorch the foliage.

ater: Heavy consumption of water in
mmer; less in autumn and winter.
ould never be allowed to dry out
mpletely. Water may be put into
base dish and the water which has
t been absorbed emptied after half an
ur.

ght: Thrives in both light and shade.
hen kept warm during the winter
ould have as well-lit a location as pos-
le so as to avoid long, etiolated
oots.

at: Normal room temperature.

: Will stand dry room air, but it is
 well to sprinkle during the hot sea-
.

-potting: Early spring.

opagation: By division in the spring
oots which are not too large.

sts: Snails and slugs.

Helxine soleirolii

Pilea nummulariifolia

Pilea nummulariifolia

Gunpowder plant

Habitat: West Indies.

Growth: Creeping plant with scabrous,
yellowy-green leaves and small, pale
green flowers, the anthers of which,
on ripening, spring into an upright
position and eject a cloud of dust
into the air, whence the common
name.

Use: Hanging-bowl plant for a shaded
room.

Soil: Standard potting mixture.

Feeding: 3 grams of fertiliser per litre
(1 oz. per gallon) of water every week
(March–September).

Water: Summer, normal watering; winter, moderate.

Light: Full or half shade.

Heat: Room temperature should not be
too high; winter, best at minimum
15° C. (60° F.).

Air: Air should for preference be
humid in spring, otherwise normal room
air.

Re potting: February.

Propagation: By cuttings in the spring.

Pests: Slugs and snails.

Other species: See below.

Pilea cadierei

Pilea cadierei

Aluminium plant

Habitat: Vietnam.
Growth: 30-cm. (12-in.)-high foliage plant. The large, dark green leaves have 4 rows of aluminium-coloured spots and, between these, 3 distinct longitudinal stripes.
Culture: As for *Pilea nummulariifolia*. Must be cut back every spring in order to produce compact plants.
Varieties: 'Silver tree' and 'Nana Bronze'.

Piperaceae

Peperomia argyreia
(Sandersii)   (51)

Rugby Football plant or **Watermelon Peperomia**

Habitat: South America.
Growth: Succulent stems with thick, fleshy, heart-shaped, dark green leaves, which have silvery-white stripes between their curved longitudinal veins. The flowers are gathered into spikes which are like mice tails.
Use: Undemanding indoor plant.
Soil: Soilless mixture.
Feeding: 2 grams of fertiliser per litre ($\frac{1}{2}$ oz. per gallon) of water every 2 weeks (March–September).
Water: Summer, normal watering; winter, keep very dry.

Light: Shade, for example in a windo facing north.
Heat: Normal room temperature; w not stand temperatures below minimu 5° C. (40° F.).
Air: Likes a high degree of humidity.
Re-potting: Early spring, in pans. Pl at the same depth as before. Av damaging the brittle stems and lea when re-potting.
Propagation: By leaf cuttings.
Pests: Snails and slugs.
Other species: See below.

Peperomia arifolia

Growth: Pointed, heart-shaped, pl dark green leaves. Many light flo spikes at the tips of the shoots.
Use and culture: As for *Peperomia ar reia*.

Peperomia caperata

Growth: Small, wavy, wrinkled lea Dense, firm white flower spike, whic rather like a pipe-cleaner. Flowers b in spring and in autumn, but is not p ticularly durable indoors.
Culture: As for *Peperomia argyreia*.

Peperomia arifolia

Peperomia caperata

peromia griseoargentea

owth: Silvery-grey, marbled leaves
h distinctive veins.
e and culture. As for *Peperomia argy-*
a.

peromia obtusifolia (52)

owth: Sturdy, dark green leaves,
ped like magnolia leaves with yel-
y-white, irregularly distributed
ts. The plant may be rejuvenated by
opping in the spring.
e and culture: As for *Peperomia argy-*
-. The 'U.S.A.' variety is to be pre-
-ed

ocromia subtrinervis (53)

owth: Thin, reddish stems with light
-n leaves. Good hanging plant.
ture: As for *Peperomia argyreia.*

er nigrum

per

itat: Malabar Coast.
owth: Slow-growing, climbing plant
shiny, heart-shaped leaves. The
s provide black and white pepper,
the flowers do not develop under
or culture.

Use: Attractive climbing plant in large
flower windows.
Soil: Soilless mixture.
Feeding: 2 grams of fertiliser per litre
($\frac{1}{2}$ oz. per gallon) of water every 2 weeks
(March–September).
Water: Even watering the whole year
round.
Light: Full or half-shade; also thrives in
windows facing north.
Heat: Normal room temperatures, but
not below minimum 12° C. (55° F.).
Air: Ordinary dry room air.
Re-potting: February, when the new
shoots are to be seen.
Propagation: By shoot cuttings over
high base heat.
Pests: Red spider mites.
NOTE: White, pearl-like precipitations
on the undersides of the leaves are a
natural phenomenon and not a sign of
disease.

Proteaccae

Grevillea robusta

Habitat: Australia, where the plant is
the holy tree of the Aborigines. Here,
it grows to a height of 30 m. (nearly
100 ft.) and is the host plant for the
epiphytic *Platycerium bifurcatum.*

Piper nigrum

Grevillea robusta

Growth: Slender trunk with light, strongly indented, fern-like leaves.
Use: Best as a 1-year indoor plant in a light window. Older plants grow too big for indoor culture, but are very suitable for conservatories, possibly as tub plants which can be moved out of doors in the summer to be kept on a balcony, on a terrace or in a patio.
Soil: Soilless mixture.
Feeding: 4 grams of fertiliser per litre (1¼ oz. per gallon) of water every 2 weeks (March–September). Winter, no nourishment at all.
Water: Regular watering the whole year round. Both excessive water and extreme drought will damage the roots and may cause the death of the plant.
Light: Will stand large amounts of light. The leaves easily take on a bronzy tinge, however, if exposed to intense sunlight.
Heat: Even warmth the whole year round. Will not stand temperatures which are too high, but on the other hand will not tolerate temperatures below a minimum 15°C. (60°F.).
Air: Dry indoor air.
Re-potting: Early spring, when growth begins.
Propagation: By seed.
Pests: Mealy bug, red spider.

Caryophyllaceae

Dianthus caryophyllus (5

Carnation

Growth: Sturdy stems with dense le rosettes and abundant flowers. Alm all colours are represented in the ran of varieties. Delicate fragrance.
Use: Formerly an indoor plant f rooms which were not too warm in t winter. Can be kept in the garden duri the summer in a sunny place.
Soil: Soilless mixture, with lar amounts of gravel or sand added. Go drainage in the pot.
Feeding: 2 grams of fertiliser per li (½ oz. per gallon) of water every 3 wee in the summer-time.
Water: Relatively dry. Never water the base dish.
Light: Full light, preferably in a sur spot.
Heat: Out of doors in summer; in w ter, best at minimum 12–15°C. (5 60°F.).
Air: Will stand dry air.
Re-potting: The end of summer, after stay in the garden.
Propagation: By planting cuttings damp sand as early as possible in spring, which will produce firm, ge flowering plants for September.

Nyctaginaceae

Bougainvillea glabra (

Habitat: Brazil.
Growth: Powerful, thorny climb plant with 3 inconspicuous flowers each inflorescence, which is surroun by 3 brightly coloured bracts in re violet. Flowering in March–July.
Use: Trellis plant for large-s arrangements, e.g. large flower wind or conservatories. Tub plants can placed out of doors in a warm spot ing the summer.
Soil: Strong garden soil with s added. (John Innes No. 3.)

eding: 2 grams of fertiliser per litre oz. per gallon) every week ebruary–September). Has a strong petite, so alternate indoor plant urishment with ammonium sulphate.
ater: To be kept well watered during growth period, but drier in the rest- period from September to January.
ght: As sunny as possible.
at: Normal temperatures; winter, at minimum 10–12° C. (50– F.).
: Spraying when growth begins in the ly spring, otherwise dry air.
potting: January, in slightly larger s. Take care with the thorns.
pagation: By cuttings in the early ng over strong base heat.
s: Scale insects, mealy bug.
E: Flowers are shed with excessive tuations in temperature. The lilac n fares best in indoor culture.

oceae

yroderma testiculare   (56)

itat: South Africa.
wth: A succulent, the appearance of h tones with the siliceous stone, cal- ous tufa and quartz fragments of its undings, from which it is difficult istinguish the plant. At times of rain plant absorbs large quantities of r, which is stored in cells in the s which are above the surface and h it uses during the long period of ght. The white, yellow, red or ve flowers emerge at the beginning ie rainy season which follows, but unfold properly in full sunshine.
   Ideal indoor plant, which 'takes of itself'. The pot is buried in sand box placed in a south-facing win-

   Half sand, half soilless mixture. ·5. Good drainage.
ing: Never.
r: October–February: once every 3 s, so that the soil balls do not dry

out entirely. March–April: every 3 days, when growth is about to begin. May–September: generous watering in hot weather every day, otherwise as required. Never moisten the plant it- self.
Light: Window facing south in direct sunlight.
Heat: Summer, as warm as possible; winter, best at only 6° C. (42° F.). Will not stand frost. Warm winter will cause flowering to fail.
Air: Dry indoor air with sprinkling necessary during summer. Avoid draughts.
Re-potting: Never.
Propagation: By division or seed.
NOTE: Growth is regulated by watering.
Other species: See below.

Conophytum springbokensis   (57)

Growth: Yellow flowers in August. After flowering has ceased the surface of the plant shrivels up and a new pair of leaves develops from the centre.
Culture requirements: Resting period, to be kept warm and dry, April–August. Otherwise, as for *Argyroderma testicu- lare.*

Faucaria tigrina   (58)

Growth: Edges of the leaves densely covered with sharp 'teeth'. Yellow flowers.
Culture requirements: As for *Argyro- derma testiculare.*

Fenestraria rhopalophylla   (59)

Growth: Club-shaped plant with a trans- parent 'window' at the top, through which the light penetrates to the inner cells of the plant. In nature it will stand being buried in sand as long as the 'window' is kept free.
Culture requirements: As for *Argyro- derma testiculare.*

Lithops pseudotruncatella (60)

Growth: Ball-shaped plant with a narrow slit at its centre, from which the flower grows in the summer.
Culture requirements: Should be kept dry in winter and somewhat warmer than *Argyroderma testiculare*, otherwise the same.

Pleiospilos bolusii (61)

Growth: Angular plant with irregularly distributed spots. The flowers are yellow, orange and magenta.
Culture requirements: As for *Argyroderma testiculare*.

In the following descriptions, the term *areole* refers to the area on the leaves (pads) of cactus from which spring spines, bristles, glochids, hairs or wool. *Glochids* are the easily detachable, barbed spines found on many areoles, which are so painful a feature of some cacti, notably *Opuntia* spp.

Cactaceae

Cacti

Habitat: The cactus family covers some 10,000 species, virtually all of them originally from America, mainly the desert regions of Arizona and Mexico, and the Andes Mountains in Bolivia and Peru.
Growth: Cacti make excellent indoor plants. Not least their ability to store water and withstand long periods of drought makes them highly suitable for cultivation in a window. The roots are thick and sturdy and lie just below the surface of the soil, so that pots and dishes should be very flat ones. In nature the root network is able to absorb large quantities of water in a short time during tropical showers, but cannot stand constant moisture. The fleshy stems are designed to convey and store water. Since there are, as a rule, no leaves the

stems assume their functions, provid[ing] for evaporation and absorption of c[ar]bon dioxide. A layer of wax on [the] surface skin protects against too m[uch] evaporation. Otherwise the stem is p[ro]tected by the areoles, small patches w[ith] tufts of hair, bristles, glochids or spi[nes]. Cacti must have reached a certain [size] before they can flower. The flowers h[ave] a dense ring of petals in bright colo[urs] which encloses a halo of stamens. [The] individual flower often has a very sh[ort] life. The flowers of many types hav[e a] delicate, almost soporific fragran[ce]. Certain types have attractive, red, lo[ng-] lasting soft fruits, others edible fruits. *Use:* Cacti are easy indoor plants wh[ich] require a minimum of attention. T[hey] can be cultivated with other succule[nts] such as *Agave, Argyroderma* [and] *Echeveria*, but, on the other hand, t[hey] are difficult with other indoor pla[nts]. Every now and then cacti become [very] fashionable, and the large number [of] species cultivated make them hi[ghly] suitable as collector's pieces. All c[acti] have a number of culture requirem[ents] in common, which are described be[low] while special requirements are indic[ated] under the description of the species [con]cerned.
Soil: Light, porous, half sand, half [a] less mixture. pH 6–7. Arrange for [suffi]cient drainage in the form of char[coal,] shell grit or coarse gravel in the bo[ttom] of the pot in order to avoid linge[ring] moisture.
Feeding: Young plants should no[t be] given any nourishment. Older plan[ts: 1] gram of superphosphate + 1 gra[m of] potassium sulphate per litre of w[ater] ($\frac{1}{4}$ oz. of each per gallon) every [week] from June to July. The rest of the y[ear] no nourishment. No nitrogen ferti[lizer] and no ordinary indoor plant ferti[lizer] containing nitrogen.
Water: November–March: older p[lants] must be kept completely dry. Y[oung] plants should be given a little w[ater] every 2 weeks, so that they do [not]

come shrivelled. The hotter the en-
onment, the more water is needed.
ril–May: Let the pot stand deep in
ter for a few hours, and then allow
water to drip off completely. Subse-
ently, give calcium-free water
inwater) once a week. June–October:
ater 2–3 times per week, especially in
and bright weather. Water should
o be sprayed over the plant itself, but
uld not be allowed to remain in the
e dish. Place sand or gravel around
neck of the root just at the surface of
soil in order to guard against rot.

ht: As light as possible, preferably
sunlight in a window facing south.
ll not thrive on a shelf in a dark
m.

at: November–March: Best tempera-
e, minimum 6–8°C. (43–46°F.),
ugh some types thrive in tempera-
es up to 12°C. (54°F.). The hardiest
es will survive at ordinary room tem-
atures, if at the same time they stand
he light and are watered from time to
e. April–October: minimum 15–
C. (60–80°F.).

As dry as possible. Centrally
ted air is quite suitable. If left out in
garden during the summer, must be
ected by glass or plastic during long
ods of rain. Avoid draughts.

otting: Only when the parts above
surface of the soil have filled the pot.
rubber gloves when re-potting.

agation: The seeds of many types
be purchased. Sow during spring or
mer in dishes covered by glass or
thene. Cuttings must be taken with
harp knife, and the cut surface
wed to dry out for a couple of weeks
re the cutting is planted into sand.
ti with many side growths can be
agated by division, possibly at the
e time as re-potting. Finally, weaker
ties with small root networks can
rafted on to firmly rooted pillar
, best in warm, damp forcing
es or flower windows in June–July.
ts may be handled during trans-

Aporocactus flagelliformis

planting by holding the ends of a paper
collar wrapped around the plant.
NOTE: Spines in fingers may be removed
with tweezers or by dripping wax from a
burning candle on to the wounded spot.
The solidified layer of wax will remove
the thorn from the skin.
Species: See below.

Aporocactus flagelliformis

Rat-tail Cactus

Habitat: Mexico.
Growth: Long, pendulous shoots, densely
covered with small thorns. Large
crimson-pink flowers in the spring.
Use: Good indoor plant, best as a hanging plant in a suspended bowl or grafted
on to a tall pillar cactus.
Special culture requirements: Must be
kept warm and light during winter and
not allowed to dry up completely. More
water and warmth from February
onwards. Concerning culture requirements in general, see *Cacti.*

Cephalocereus senilis

Cephalocereus senilis

Old Man

Habitat: Mexico.
Growth: Slow-growing pillar cactus, densely covered with yellow spines and a thick coat of white, silk-soft hair.
Special culture requirements: Place sand around the root neck, as the roots are weak and rot easily when too much water is given. Will last many years, if it is kept in a light, dry and cool spot. Likes full sunlight in a window facing south. Concerning culture requirements in general, see *Cacti*.
NOTE: Dirty hair can be washed with soapflakes (*not* detergent), provided it is rinsed and dried thoroughly afterwards.

Echinocactus grusonii (62)

Mother-in-law's Chair

Habitat: Mexico.
Growth: Large globe with clearly defined ribs and strong, yellow-gold spines. Young plants have ribs divided into warts, like *Mammillaria hidalgensis*. The small, yellow flowers, which grow in great profusion, are unlikely to be produced except under outdoor tropical conditions or very good greenhouse cultivation.

196

Special culture requirements: As clo as possible to a window facing sou Should spend the winter at minim 8° C. (45° F.). Must be re-potted f quently and always in the spring. C cerning cultural requirements in gene see *Cacti*.

Echinopsis eyriesii

Habitat: Argentina and Uruguay.
Growth: Globe-shaped, 20 cm. (8 in. cross-section. Sharp ribs with w felted areoles bearing sharp spi Flowers up to 25 cm. (10 in.) lc open, white and fragrant; flowers only a few hours.
Special culture requirements: Flower is best attained by removing side sho Placed in half-shade during flowerin June–July. During winter must be k dry at minimum 5° C. (40° F.). C cerning culture requirements in gene see *Cacti*.
NOTE: Has been cultivated for over years. A reliable plant in any cactus lection.

Mamillaria hidalgensis (

Habitat: Mexico.
Growth: Globe-cactus with four cr patterned, attractive spines on wart projections, arranged in spiral rows. flowers are rose-red, the buds develo

Echinopsis eyriesii

Opuntia clavarioïdes

the axils—the spaces between the
…rts—when these have reached a cer-
…n age. The flowers are thus always at
…ertain distance from the centre of the
…nt. Flowers in summer.
…: Good indoor plant in full sunlight.
…ecial culture requirements: Very sen-
…ve to damp soil. Make sure, there-
…, that the pot soil is well drained and
… a high content of gravel. Protect the
… neck against lingering moisture
…h gravel. To be kept dry at a mini-
…m 8° C. (45° F.) during winter. Con-
…ing culture requirements in general,
…Cacti.

…untia phaeacantha (*form*)   (64)

…bitat: Cool regions in North and
…th America.
…wth: Round or oval, flat shoots with
…ly divided tufts of loosely mounted
…ow glochids, bearing pointed barbs
…ch easily attach themselves to
…hes and skin. The yellow flowers
…rge from the edges of the shoots
…s).
…: Very suitable for rooms and con-
…atories.
…cial culture requirements: Best at
…peratures which are not too high.
… be left to spend the summer in the

garden. Concerning culture requirements in general, see *Cacti*.
Other species: See below.

Opuntia clavarioïdes (*var.* Monstrosa)

Growth: Greenish-brown shoots with
white thorns on the crowded areoles.
Uneven growth with finger- or hand-
shaped protuberances.
Culture requirements: As for *Opuntia
phaeacantha*. Can be grafted on to
Opuntia cylindrica.

Opuntia cylindrica

Growth: Vigorous, tall-growing *Opuntia*
species, best for a conservatory.
Culture requirements: As for *Opuntia
phaeacantha*.

Opuntia ficus-indica
Prickly Pear

Growth: Vigorous *Opuntia* species,
which is used in Southern Europe as an
effective hedge plant. When out of con-
trol, it is a troublesome weed. The fruit
is edible when the glochid-covered skin
is removed.
Culture requirements: As for *Opuntia
phaeacantha*.

Opuntia tuna

Growth: Vigorous, flat shoots with stiff,
yellow-brown spines. Large, pale yellow
flowers.
Culture requirements: As for *Opuntia
phaeacantha*.

Rebutia minuscula

Habitat: Mountainous regions in
Argentina and Bolivia.
Growth: Small globular shape with
spiral ribs. Many red flowers, mainly in
May.

Rebutia minuscula

Use: Rewarding indoor plant for a window-sill.
Special culture requirements: Winter: very little water, but enough to prevent the plant from drying up. Spring: a lot of water while the buds are forming. Summer: a lot of water, and half-shade. Concerning culture requirements in general, see *Cacti*.

Selenicereus grandiflorus (65)

Night-flowering Cereus

Habitat: Haïti.
Growth: Climbing, many-branched plant; pentagonal, dark green shoots, with short spines and aerial roots on some of the shoots. Large flowers, 30 cm. (12 in.) long and 30 cm. (12 in.) in cross-section, which are golden-brown on the outside and pure white inside. Very delicate fragrance, given off during darkness, and the flower only lasts for a few hours. The plant will not usually flower until it is 8 years old.
Use: Climbing plant in a room or winter garden. Ornamental value, apart from the flower, is debatable.
Special culture requirements: Summer: sunshine, heat, plenty of water and spraying. May, under certain circumstances, be kept out of doors in summer. Winter, minimum 10° C. (50° F.) in a light growth location; water sparingly. Concerning culture requirements in general, see *Cacti*.
Other species: See below.

Selenicereus pteracanthus

Growth: Not as vigorous as *Sele cereus grandiflorus*, but better suited indoor culture. Flowers during plant's fifth year of life. Other cult requirements as above.

Schlumbergera gaertneri

Easter Cactus

Habitat: Brazil.
Growth: Very similar, with its flat, s mented, leaf-like shoots, to *Schlu bergera bridgesii*. Continued grow and the development of buds takes pl from a long areole at the tip of e; shoot. The flowers are wheel-shaped a brilliant red in colour. Flowering per March–April.
Use: Good indoor plant. Considera easier to bring to flower than the abo mentioned species. Not sensitive to pot being turned or moved in the v dow.
Culture: May–September: Gentle sh; moderate watering, temperature above minimum 25° C. (80° F.) and quent spraying. Never direct sunli October–November: Cool (minim 10° C. (50° F.)) and dry in order to mote the formation of buds. Decemb February: In January the tempera

Schlumbergera gaertneri

Rhipsalis houlletiana

Rhipsalis houlletiana

Habitat: Tropical rain forests in South America.
Growth: Flat, articulated, leaf-like, green shoots, growing up to a metre (3 ft.) in length, with sharp teeth and overhanging growth. The unattractive yellow-green flowers grow in great profusion.
Use: Hanging plant which is grown in small baskets or orchid baskets, as for orchids. Especially good in a conservatory, porch or greenhouse.

Schlumbergera bridgesii (67)

Christmas Cactus

Habitat: Tropical rain forests in Brazil.
Growth: Upright or more or less hanging growth. Flat, leaf-like green segments with flowers at their tips. The hanging flowers are dark red with several rings of petals. Frequently grafted on *Selenicereus grandiflorus* in order to develop trunked varieties. The plant's own root network is weak, and will not stand too much water, but must not be allowed to dry out.
Use: Good indoor plant, suitable as a hanging plant. Both *Schlumbergera gaertneri* and *Rhipsalidopsis rosea* are easier, however.
Culture: April–June: Light and moist, but not in direct sunshine. Spraying in hot weather, plenty of water and occasional nourishment. July–August: During the resting period at the height of the summer, the plant must be kept completely dry, in order to promote the development of the buds. September–December: Cool room temperature, best at minimum 15–18° C. (60–65° F.), but not below 12° C. (54° F.); water sparingly but spray frequently. When the buds emerge, give slightly larger amounts of water. The plant must not be moved or turned, and fluctuations in temperature are undesirable. January–

be raised to about 18° C. (65° F.), following which the buds will begin to appear. May–June: Flowering period with somewhat larger amounts of water, temperature about 20° C. (70° F.), and occasional spraying.
Soil: Leaf mould mixed with sand.
NOTE: Shedding segments, attributable as a rule to fluctuating temperature.

Rhipsalidopsis rosea (66)

Habitat: Brazil.
Growth: Hanging stem with flat, articulated leaf-like shoots around it, like *Schlumbergera bridgesii*. The flowers are large, wheel-shaped and slightly hanging. Varieties with varnish-red, light red and violet flowers. Flowering period March–September.
Use: Suitable for window-sills, or as a hanging-bowl plant. Easier to cultivate, has a lot more flowers than the above-mentioned species.
Culture: Moist, humus-rich soil (soilless culture). Summer: Evenly moist, light and sunny. During the flowering period, frequent spraying and watering. Winter: light and cool (minimum 10° C. (50° F.)). Should be re-potted early in spring, in small pots.

March: After flowering has ceased, 2 months' rest, during which the plant should be kept dry, light and cool (minimum 10° C. (50° F.)).
Soil: Loam mixed with sand most suitable.
NOTE: If allowed to dry out or given too much water, if moved or turned or subjected to excessive temperature fluctuations, the plant may shed its buds.

Epiphyllum hybridum (68)

Habitat: Tropical rain forests in Central and South America.
Growth: Epiphyte with relatively weak roots and flat, leaf-like shoots with tufts of soft needles on the edges. Often short aerial roots in the joints. Flowers are large, white, light red or dark red with a thick tuft of stamens in the centre, and only emerge isolated from the edges of the leaf-branches in April–June.
Use: Easily cultivated indoor plant with no ornamental value outside the flowering season. Can spend the summer out of doors in a shady spot.
Culture: Light and cool growth location, moist soil, plenty of water and spraying in hot weather, also after flowering has ceased. Give plenty of water and weekly application of nourishment until August. Should spend the winter at a minimum 8–12° C. (45–55° F.) and have enough water to avoid shrivelling up of the shoots. High winter temperature promotes the formation of shoots which do not flower and are removed in spring. *Re-potting:* Every 2 or 3 years in light soil, rich in humus (leaf mould with peat or sand added, possibly loamless compost).

Lauraceae

Laurus nobilis

Bay Tree

Growth: Bush or tree with evergreen, coriaceous leaves and small, yellowy-

Laurus nobilis

white flowers. The leaves contain aromatic flavouring substance.
Use: Tub plant for ornamental purpos Should spend the winter in a cool, fre free conservatory, summer out of do on a terrace or in a patio (Ap October).
Soil: Strong, nourishing loam v bonemeal (Animix) added, possibly s less mixture.
Feeding: 5 grams of fertiliser per l ($1\frac{1}{2}$ oz. per gallon) of water per w during the growth period.
Water: Plenty during growth period winter, just enough to prevent the mass from drying out altogether.
Light: Will stand some shade. L during winter.
Heat: Summer, normal temperat winter, minimum 5° C. (40° F.).
Air: Spraying during the gro period.
Re-potting: Only when the root n completely fills the tub. Plenty of b nourishment with weekly addition preferable to changing the soil.
Pests: Greenfly, mealy-bugs, scale sects.
NOTE: Too much water in the wi will cause yellowing and shedding leaves.

Passifloraceae

Passiflora coerulea (69)

Passion Flower

Habitat: Central America.

Growth: Climbing plant with palmate leaves, tendrils and strange flower structures, individual parts of which have been associated with items from the story of the Passion of Christ. It is said that the ring of wire-like nectaries is the crown of thorns, the 5 stamens are Christ's wounds, the pistil is the chalice and the triple stigma the nails in the cross. The petals in the white variety symbolise the Saviour's innocence, and the petals of the blue variety take their colour from the Virgin Mary's sky blue cloak. Flowering period is July–September. The single flower only lasts for a day; the fruit is pretty and edible.

Use: Attractive climbing plant in a light window or a conservatory, or in a warm spot out of doors. May be cultivated as an annual or perennial plant, though it will not flower the same year as seed is sown.

Soil: Strong garden soil with bonemeal added. Not soilless mixture.

Feeding: 3 grams of fertiliser per litre (½ oz. per gallon) of water, every week April–September.

Water: Plenty during the summer; in winter, only a little, but the soil should not be allowed to dry out completely.

Light: Very demanding, but should be lightly shaded from scorching midday sun.

Heat: Moderate temperature; winter, not at minimum 8°C. (45°F.).

Air: Damp air at the beginning of growth in spring.

Repotting: Early spring, before the new roots develop.

Cutting: In spring the flowering shoots of the previous year are cut back, down to 6–8 buds.

Propagation: By layers, cuttings and seeds.

Pests: Red spider mites.
Varieties: 'Constance Elliott' (white) and 'Empress Eugenie' (violet).
Other species: See below.

Passiflora coccinea

Growth: Small, red star flowers.
Use and culture: As for *Passiflora coerulea.* Winter temperature minimum 10–12°C. (50–55°F.).

Passiflora racemosa

Growth: Red flowers in small clusters.
Use and culture: As for *Passiflora coerulea.*

Begoniaceae

Begonia cheimantha
(B. socotrana × B. dregei) (70)

'Gloire de Lorraine'

Growth: Dense plant with succulent, fragile roots, light green leaves and white, pale red and plain red flowers in great profusion.

Use: Originally, a distinct Christmas bloom, which is now cultivated from the early autumn to late spring. Cheap and easy ornamental plant which, with good care, will last for many years in indoor culture. Cut flowers are highly ornamental, and last a long time in water.

Soil: Soilless mixture, possibly half garden soil and half peat. pH 7.

Feeding: 1 gram of fertiliser per litre (½ oz. per gallon) of water, every week during the growth period.

Water: The pot soil should be kept evenly moist. Best watered through a base dish; excess water should be poured away half an hour after watering. When watered too sparingly, buds and flowers are shed.

Light: Likes a light spot but away from direct sunshine.

Heat: Should be gradually accustomed

Begonia socotranum x tuberhybrida

to room temperature, from minimum 12°C. (55°F.) in October to minimum 18°C. (65°F.) in mid-winter. Higher temperatures cause dropping of flowers and prevent the development of new buds.

Air: Fresh air counteracts attack from mildew.

Re-potting: Re-pot older plants carefully, when the roots fill the pots.

Cutting: After flowering has ceased, cut back the top so that the plant can flower again.

Propagation: By cuttings in a forcing house.

Diseases: Mildew, especially in still, damp air. Shedding of buds and flowers when soil is too dry and temperature too high.

Varieties: 'Marina' (pink), 'Marietta' (pink) and 'Regent' (pale pink).

Other species: See below.

Begonia socotrana tuberhybrida

Growth: Smaller than *Begonia cheimantha*, but has larger flowers. Use and culture otherwise the same.

Varieties: 'Elatior' (crimson), 'Baardses Favorite' (bright red), 'President' (red, double), 'Oranje Zon' (orange) an 'Exquisite' (pink).

Begonia rex-cultorum   (7)

Growth: Short, downy stems and leave on long stalks with attractive pattern Small, dirty-white flowers in cluster February–April. Found in a large va iety of types and hybrids with differe leaf patterns in red, silvery-grey ar green.

Use: Long-lasting indoor plant.

Soil: Soilless mixture.

Feeding: 2 grams of fertiliser per lit ($\frac{1}{2}$ oz. per gallon) of water every wee February–September.

Water: Water evenly but sparingly du ing the resting period from October January.

Light: Half-shade, never direct su shine.

Heat: Normal room temperatu (approx. 20°C. (70°F.)). Sensitive temperatures below 10°C. (50°F.).

Air: Damp air with frequent spraying the spring.

Re-potting: After flowering has ceas in May.

Propagation: By leaf cuttings.

Begonia argenteo-guttata

ests: Thrips in dry environments, red
spider mites in sunlight.

Begonia argenteo-guttata

Growth: Creeping, succulent, downy
stems. The wing-shaped leaves are
bronze-coloured with silvery-grey markings. Pink flowers in hanging inflores-
ences.
Use: Good indoor plant in a warm
room, conservatory or hothouse.
Culture: As for *Begonia rex-cultorum.*
Other species of fibrous rooted begonia:
see below.

Begonia corallina

Growth: Shiny leaves with red undersides. Coral red, hanging flowers.
Use and culture: As for *Begonia rex-*
cultorum. Needs a lot of warmth.
Hybrids: A good hybrid is 'President
Carnot', with tall, robust stems, reddish
leaves with white markings and crimson
flower clusters.

Begonia credneri

Growth: Vigorous growth. Downy,
olive-green leaves with dark patterns.

Begonia corallina

Begonia fuchsioides

Light red flowers in large clusters the
whole year round.
Use and culture: As for *Begonia rex-*
cultorum. Will stand more sunlight than
the other Begonias.
Varieties: 'Berlin', 'Dresden' and 'Stutt-
gart' with downy leaves having red
undersides, and white flowers.

Begonia erythrophylla

Growth: The leaves are wax-like and
olive-green with red undersides. The
flowers are a delicate pink in the winter.
Use and culture: As for *Begonia rex-*
cultorum. Will stand ordinary room
temperatures.

Begonia fuchsioides

Growth: Branched, slightly pendulous
stems. Leaves are a glistening dark
green. Pink flowers in summer and
autumn.
Use and culture: As for *Begonia rex-*
cultorum. Will stand ordinary room
temperatures.

Begonia manicata

Begonia manicata

Growth: Has rosettes of red down on stems and at base of leaves. Tall stems with pale pink flower clusters in the winter.

Use and culture: As for *Begonia rex-cultorum.*

Begonia masoniana 'Iron Cross'

Growth: Tough, embossed leaves with dark patterns like 'iron crosses'. Older leaves are silvery-grey with red down. The flowers are greenish-white with red down.

Use and culture: As for *Begonia rex-cultorum.*

Begonia semperflorens

Growth: Low compact plant with small white, pink or red flowers the whole year round.

Use: For planting out in a flower-bed or a balcony-box, but also suitable as an indoor plant in not too warm a room.

Soil: Soilless mixture.

Feeding: 3 grams of fertiliser per litre of water (1 oz. per gallon) every week (February–November).

Water: Normal watering the whole year round.

Light: Will stand sunshine, but shou be slightly shaded in the height of t summer.

Heat: Fares best at minimum 12–15° (55–60° F.).

Air: Will stand very dry room air.

Re-potting: Spring, when the roots the pot.

Cutting: Prune tops when flowering too meagre.

Propagation: By seeding.

Varieties: 'Harzperle', 12 cm. (4 i tall, pink flowers, red leaves; 'Pand 12 cm. (4 in.) tall, red; 'Tausendschö 15 cm. (5 in.) tall, pink and wh variant; 'Carmen', 20 cm. (8 in.) t plain pink; 'Albert Martin', 35 cm. (in.) tall, purple-red.

Begonia tuberhybrida   (7

Growth: Thick, flat tubers, slan leaves and large numbers of single double flowers in shades of white, y low, orange and red.

Use: Primarily a summer flower for garden, balcony-box or flower-bowl, can also be cultivated as a summ flowering indoor plant in light and a windows.

Soil: Soilless mixture.

Begonia semperflorens

eeding: 2 grams of fertiliser per litre
(¼ oz. per gallon) of water every 2 weeks
(April–August).

Water: The soil balls must not be
allowed to dry out. The dry tuber should
be kept in dry peat litter or sand during
the winter.

Light: Window facing south.

Heat: Normal room temperature.

Air: Fresh, not too damp.

Re-potting: The tuber is potted in
February for forcing at even heat.

Propagation: By seeding or side tubers.
(Cuttings are quite easy.)

Disease: Mildew.

Varieties: There are a large number of
varieties, single or double, in many
bright colours, for example, 'Frau
Helene Harms' (yellow), 'Flamboyant'
(red) and 'Pendula' (red), the last-
mentioned being a hanging plant and
suitable for a suspended basket.

eaceae

Camellia japonica (73)

Habitat: Mountain forests in Eastern
Asia.

Growth: Branching bush with attractive
coriaceous leaves and large, single or
double flowers in white, pink or red.

Use: Excellent plant in cool conservatories or unheated but frost-free verandas. Only successful as an indoor
plant if it is kept constantly in the same
place and not turned.

Soil: Soilless mixture or lime-free loam
with peat and sand added. Good drain

Feeding: 2 grams of ammonium sulphate, alternated with 2 grams normal
plant fertiliser per litre (½ oz. per gallon
in each case) of water every 2 weeks,
January–July.

Water: The amount of moisture in the
soil should be kept constant the
whole time, but the soil must never be
thoroughly wet. Only use rainwater or
some other soft water, or add 2 parts per

Oxalis deppei

thousand of ammonium sulphate to normal tap water on each watering.

Light: Light window facing east or
west, without direct, scorching midday
sun.

Heat: Buds form best in January at minimum 18° C. (65° F.). When the buds
are large and swollen, the temperature
should be reduced to minimum 8° C.
(46° F.) for a few weeks. The flowers
emerge when the plant is replaced in a
warm environment (minimum 15° C.
(60° F.)). Summer, normal room temperature; from October to December,
cooler once more (minimum 8° C.
(46° F.)).

Air: Damp air, especially while buds are
forming. Spray daily.

Re-potting: After flowering has ceased
in the early summer.

Propagation: By cuttings or grafting in
specialised nurseries.

Diseases: Bud drop is caused by excessive heat, temperature fluctuations, too
much soil moisture (or excessive dry-
ness) or removal of the plant.

Oxalidaceae

Oxalis deppei

Habitat: Mexico.

Growth: Tuberous, edible rhizomes,
four-bladed, clover-like leaves with dark
ribbon patterns and tile-red flowers.

Use: Undemanding indoor plant.
Soil: Soilless mixture.
Feeding: 2 grams of fertiliser per litre ($\frac{1}{2}$ oz. per gallon) of water every 2 weeks (March–August).
Water: Plenty during growth period, very sparing during the resting period in the winter.
Light: Window facing east or west.
Heat: Normal room temperature.
Air: Dry room air.
Re-potting: Early spring.
Propagation: By side tubers, which are separated from the parent plant at the same time as re-potting.

Geraniaceae

Pelargonium × domesticum   (74)

Regal Pelargonium

Growth: Low, branching bush with sharp-toothed, downy leaves. Large, white, pink or red flowers with spots, veins or flames in various colours, collected into round inflorescences. Flowers during the whole of the summer.
Use: Perennial plant with cool wintering on a light veranda, in a conservatory or other such unheated, frost-free indoor location. May also be used out of doors in a balcony box or plant tub during the summer. The plant is most attractive, and flowers most abundantly in its third year.
Soil: Soilless mixture or other soil rich in nutrients. pH 5–6·5.
Feeding: 5 grams of fertiliser per litre ($1\frac{1}{2}$ oz. per gallon) of water every week (April–August).
Water: Plenty during growth period; resting period from August, with less water. When the new shoots begin to develop in September, start to water generously once more. From November, very dry, cool winter.
Light: As much as possible. During flowering, best placed in a window facing east or west.

Heat: Normal room temperature; wi[n]ter, minimum 8° C. (45° F.).
Air: Fresh, not enclosed and not to[o] dry.
Re-potting: Early spring, before grow[th] begins.
Cutting: Pruning after flowering h[as] ceased in August, so as to favour t[he] growth of vigorous bushy plants.
Propagation: Pruned top shoots can [be] used as cuttings, which are planted [in] moist, plain sand.
Pest: Greenfly.
Disease: Fungus on leaves is as a r[ule] due to lack of fresh air.
Varieties: 'Frühlingszauber' (pale pin[k/] reddish brown); 'Schneewittch[en]' (white/carmine); 'Glut' (cherry-re[d/] white/black spots).

Pelargonium × hortorum   (7[5])

Geranium

Habitat: South Africa.
Growth: Upright stems with round gre[en] leaves having a brown horseshoe p[at]tern. Self-coloured flowers (white, pi[nk,] mauve and red varieties) in dense infl[or]escences.
Use: Good plant for balcony boxes [or] bowls out of doors in summer. Oth[er]wise undemanding, perennial ind[oor] plant, best kept cool during winter o[n a] veranda, in a conservatory or simi[lar.] Easily satisfied plant in a warm su[nny] window facing south.
Soil: Soilless mixture.
Feeding: 5 grams of fertiliser per l[itre] ($1\frac{1}{2}$ oz. per gallon) of water every w[eek] from March to August.
Water: Summer: Normal watering. [Will] stand being kept dry for a time. Win[ter:] Dry.
Light: Will stand direct sunlight. Ple[nty] of light in winter.
Heat: Normal room temperature; w[in]ter, minimum 10° C. (50° F.).
Air: Fresh, not enclosed air.
Re-potting: Early spring, before gro[wth] begins.

tting: Late summer, after flowering
s ceased.
opagation: By cuttings from summer
uning, or cuttings from the new
owth in early spring.
rieties: 'Volkskanzler' (bright red),
nk' (deep red), 'Åvang' (salmon red).

largonium peltatum (76)

-leafed Geranium

owth: Metre-long (3-ft.) hanging
ms with elegant, ivy-like leaves.
rge influorescences in white, pink,
uve and red. One or two double var-
es.
e: Good balcony plant. Indoor hang-
-bowl plant for a room or conserva-
y. Not a climber.
il: Soilless mixture, possibly with
avel or sand added.
ding: 3 grams of fertiliser per litre
oz. per gallon) of water every week
ing the growth period.
ter: Water normally in summer,
ringly in winter.
ht: Full sunlight.
at: Summer, humid, around mini-
m 20° C. (70° F.), winter about mini-
m 10° C. (50° F.).
: Absolutely fresh, but will stand dry
m air.
potting: Early spring.
ting: After flowering has ceased, and
ore the winter resting period begins.
pagation: By cuttings in the late
mmer.
teties. 'Balkonkönigin' (pale pink),
nne d'Arc' (white), 'Cattleya'
uve), 'M. Marquis' (red).

Isaminaceae

atiens walleriana (77)

y Lizzie

itat: Tropical Africa.
wth: Herbaceous, succulent stems
fresh green leaves and single, flat
ers in white, pale red or scarlet.

Use: Undemanding, immensely prolific
indoor flower plant. Suitable for outdoor
use in the summer in a balcony box, on
a terrace or in a patio.
Soil: Soilless mixture.
Feeding: 3 grams of fertiliser per litre
(1 oz. per gallon) of water each week
(February–September). Flowering will
be too meagre if insufficient nourishment is given.
Water: Heavy consumption; during the
hot season, frequently needs to be
watered several times a day. In winter,
water more sparingly.
Light: Light shade during the summer,
not direct sunshine. Light during the
winter.
Heat: Normal room temperature. Very
warm during the winter (minimum
20° C. (70° F.)) in a light location; then
cooler (minimum 12° C. (55° F.)) with a
shadier position.
Air: Humid air. Spraying needed.
Re-potting: Early spring. Vigorous
plants possibly again in June.
Cutting: Top pruning after each major
flowering. The plant rapidly spreads
new shoots and many flower buds.
Propagation: By cuttings of pruned top
shoots, which easily strike roots in
water.
Pests: Greenfly, red spider mites.
NOTE: One of our most prolific flowering
indoor plants.

Rutaceae

Fortunella japonica (78)

Kumquat

Habitat: China.
Growth: Small tree with shiny leaves,
small, white, fragrant flowers, and small
orange-yellow, long lasting fruits, which
are edible but very bitter.
Use: The orange and lemon trees grown
in the South grow indoors well enough
but can rarely, if ever, be brought to
flower or bear fruit. On the other hand,
the Chinese Kumquat is an excellent

plant for light windows, where it flowers almost the whole year round and at the same time bears long-lasting miniature oranges.

Soil: Soilless mixture.
Feeding: 2 grams of fertiliser per litre ($\frac{1}{2}$ oz. per gallon) of water every 2 weeks (February–October).
Water: Plenty, but allow the soil to dry out between times.
Light: Full sunlight.
Heat: Normal room temperature; winter, not below minimum 10° C. (50° F.).
Air: Will stand dry room air.
Re-potting: Frequent re-potting, as growth proceeds rapidly.
Cutting: Prune back top shoots, if the plant begins to take up too much of the window.
Propagation: By top cuttings over bottom heat.
NOTE: The seeds of oranges, lemons and grapefruit can be sown in window-pots, where they quickly germinate and will make attractive, evergreen miniature plants, but—as a rule—they are unable to flower, still less bear fruit.

Tiliaceae

Sparmannia africana   (79)
African Hemp

Habitat: Africa.
Growth: Vigorous plant with lime-like, downy leaves and off-white flowers with yellow and dark red stamens. The flowering period occurs in the spring and summer.
Use: Indoor plant for large-scale requirements, e.g. a veranda or conservatory. Cannot spend the summer out of doors, since the soft leaves are destroyed in windy weather.
Soil: Soilless mixture (large pots).
Feeding: 3 grams of fertiliser per litre (1 oz. per gallon) of water every week (March–September).
Water: Plenty during the growth period; water more sparingly in winter.

Light: Full sunlight.
Heat: Summer, normal room temperature; winter, minimum 12° C. (55° F.)
Air: Will stand dry room air.
Re-potting: February, in large pots account of the vigorous root network.
Propagation: By firm top shoots in spring.
Pest: Red spider mite (yellow l spots).
Disease: Leaves turn yellow and dr when insufficient nourishment is giver

Malvaceae

Abutilon hybridum

Habitat: South America.
Growth: Small bush with 3–5 lob leaves shaped like maple leaves. Th are varieties with variegated yell leaves. The flowers are hanging b with conspicuous yellow stamens pistil in the middle. They app throughout the summer, in colours cluding white, yellow and dark purpl
Use: Good indoor plant in rooms wh are not too warm. Suitable for conser tories and verandas, and in the sum for warm terraces or patios.
Soil: Soilless mixture.
Feeding: 3 grams of fertiliser per l (1 oz. per gallon) of water every w (February–August).
Water: Summer, plenty; in winter, s ply keep the soil slightly damp.
Light: Half-shade in summer; win light.
Heat: Normal room temperature; ter, about 15° C. (60° F.) minimum.
Air: Spraying in spring, otherwise room air.
Re-potting: April, in pots which are too large. Add basic nourishment bonemeal, Peraform) when re-potting
Cutting: Trim large plants by hard p ing in April.
Propagation: Pruned top shoots rooted in damp sand.
Pests: Greenfly in dry air and draug

Malvastrum capense

d spider mites in too sunny growth
cations.

seases: Sudden changes in tempera-
re cause leaves to turn yellow and fall.
her species: See below.

utilon megapotamicum (80)

azilian Abutilon

owth: Small leaves, overhanging
anches and yellow and red lantern
wers. The *aureum* form has varie-
ed yellow foliage.
e and culture: As for *Abutilon
oridum.*

utilon striatum thompsonii (81)

ompson's Abutilon

owth: Orange-red flowers and varie-
ed yellow foliage.
e and culture; As for *Abutilon hyb-
um.*

iscus rosa-sinensis (82)

iscus

bitat: Tropics.
owth: Dense bush with fresh green
age and very large funnel-shaped
wers with yellow pistils and stamens.
ours: White, yellow, pink and red.
ible forms may be found. The indivi-
l flower only lasts for a few days.
: Good prolific indoor flower plant
light, but not warm, rooms. May be
on a warm balcony or in a similar
door location during the summer.
: Soilless mixture.
ding: 3 grams of fertiliser per litre
z. per gallon) of water, every week
ruary–August).
er: Plenty during the summer,
ewhat less in winter, but never allow
ry out completely.
t: Half-shade in summer, preferably
window facing north. As light as
ible in winter for early flowering.
t: Normal room temperature; win-
not less than 12°C. (55°F.). Fares
at minimum 20°C. (70°F.).

Air: Slightly humid air. The leaves roll up
in excessively dry air and buds are shed.
Re-potting: February.
Cutting: Prune older, larger plants in
February.
Propagation: By top cuttings from
pruned material.
Pests: Greenfly, mealy bugs, red spider
mites.
Diseases: Changing temperature and air
humidity cause shedding of buds.

Malvastrum capense

Habitat: South Africa.
Growth: Small bush with downy, slightly sticky, 3-lobed leaves, rather like
those of a gooseberry bush. The flowers
are small, pink and mallow-like.
Use: Good flowering indoor plant.
Culture: As for *Abutilon hybridum.*
Grows thin and scraggy in shade. Will
stand being thoroughly pruned in the
spring.

Euphorbiaceae

Acalypha hispida

Habitat: Tropics.
Growth: Shrubby plant with green
leaves and long red inflorescences,

Acalypha hispida

shaped like a cat's tail. Young plants with a single growth provide the biggest inflorescences.

Use: Attractive indoor plant in spring and summer. Difficult plant to bring through the winter.

Soil: Soilless mixture.

Feeding: 2 grams of fertiliser per litre ($\frac{1}{2}$ oz. per gallon) of water every 2 weeks (February–August).

Water: Evenly moist, but not too wet.

Light: Window facing east or west, not direct sunshine.

Heat: As warm as possible. Certainly not below 15°C. (60°F.).

Air: Very damp air. In central heating, the leaves roll up.

Re-potting: February, in small pots.

Cutting: The top shoots on older plants should be cut back to obtain a better spread of branches.

Propagation: By cuttings over high bottom heat.

Pests: Red spider mites in dry air.

Other species: See below.

Acalypha wilkesiana

Growth: Foliage plant with attractively marbled leaves in plain red, copper-red

and brown colours. The flowers are r worthy of special comment. There a many hybrids.

Use and culture: As for *Acalyp hispida.*

Codiaeum variegatum (8

Croton

Habitat: India. (East Indies.)

Growth: Evergreen bush with a w variety of leaf-shapes and colours green, yellow, orange and red shades.

Use: Typical tropical plant, which li a high temperature and a high degree air humidity. Best in a hot greenho or conservatory. Not so well suited rooms with dry air. Can be used as ornamental plant for short periods.

Soil: Soilless mixture.

Feeding: 3 grams of fertiliser per l (1 oz. per gallon) of water every 2 we (March–August).

Water: Normal watering. Should have too much moisture, but should be allowed to dry out completely.

Light: Window facing east or west, direct sunshine. When strongly sha the leaves turn green and lose t coloured patterns altogether.

Heat: High room temperature; wir not below minimum 18°C. (65°F.).

Air: High degree of air humidity whole year round. Frequent spraying

Re-potting: February.

Cutting: Nipping the top shoots duces bushy plants.

Propagation: By cuttings over high heat, in February.

Pests: Red spider mites, thrips, s insects, mealy-bugs.

Diseases: Leaves are shed when plant is subjected to sudden change temperature.

Euphorbia pulcherrima

Poinsettia

Habitat: Mexico.

Growth: Branching bush with slig

210

dented leaves. Small, yellowy-green
〜wers surrounded by a ring of bright
d bracts. When cut or damaged the
ant exudes a milky substance, known
latex.

〜e: Seasonal plant which is sold
〜ound Christmas-time, and with care
ll prove an excellent perennial indoor
ant. If kept in the dark for 14 hours
t of every 24 during 4 weeks, flower-
〜 can be induced at any season of the
ar.

〜il: Soilless mixture, possibly with the
dition of extra bonemeal as basic fer-
〜ser.

〜eding: 3 grams of fertiliser per litre
oz. per gallon) of water every week
〜ne—October). (Has a large appetite.)

〜ter: Plenty during the summer, and
〜vays lukewarm, never cold tap water.
〜ei flowering and until the May rest-
period, give less water by compar-
〜n. The soil must, however, not be
〜wed to dry out, otherwise the leaves
l be shed.

〜ht: Summer, half-shade, otherwise as
〜t as possible so that colour is
〜ained on the bracts.

〜t: Normal room temperature.
〜wering plants last longest at mini-
〜m 15°C. (60°F.).

〜 Best in damp air. Frequent spray-

〜potting: In May the old soil is
〜ken loose from the roots, the top is
〜 back and the plant is re-potted in
〜 which are not too large. Bleeding
〜nds on branches may be stopped by
〜ping in warm water.

〜pagation: By cuttings in sand and
〜 at minimum 20°C. (70°F.) in late
〜mer.

〜s: Red spider mites.

〜ieties: 'Paul Mikkelsen' (dark red,
〜 long-lasting), 'Annette Hogg' (dark
many branches), 'Mikkelpink' and
〜ddeldawn' (pale red), 'Mikkelwhite'
'White Ecke' (white).

〜r species: See below. Most
〜horbias (Spurges) are decorative

and undemanding indoor plants, suitable for cultivation in sunny windows in
dry air. There are a number of succulent
varieties to choose from. Globe-shaped,
or pillar-shaped, with or without cactus-
like thorns, with or without green foliage
leaves.

Euphorbia milii (85)
Crown of Thorns

Habitat: Madagascar.
Growth: Slightly twining, angular, grey-
green branches, densely covered with
long, pointed thorns. Fresh-green foliage
leaves. Coral-red bracts together with
small, greenish-yellow flowers in the
spring.
Use: First-class indoor plant in baking
hot sunshine in a south-facing position.
Very slow growth.
Soil: Soilless mixture.
Feeding: 2 grams of fertiliser per litre
($\frac{1}{4}$ oz. per gallon) every 2 weeks (April–
August).
Water: No water, January–February. A
little water on sunny days in March. The
rest of the year, moderate watering. The
soil should be left to dry out between
each watering.
Light: Full sunlight.
Heat: Normal room temperature. Will
also stand a cool winter at minimum
12°C. (55°F.).
Air: Will stand both dry and damp air.
Re-potting: At intervals of several years.
Take care with the thorns.
Cutting: May–June, to obtain the best
branch formation.
Propagation: By cuttings from older
shoots. The cut surface must be allowed
to dry in the air before grafting into
equal parts of sand and soil.
Diseases: Leaf shedding is a sign of too
low temperatures or too much moisture.
NOTE: Leaf shedding during the resting
period is normal, and new leaves appear
when the new growth period begins. Apparently dead plants are still alive if the
actual shoot tips are green.

Euphorbia erythraea

Euphorbia pugniformis (86)

Habitat: South Africa.
Growth: Succulent with white milk-sap. Snake-like side shoots spread out on all sides from the plant's globular central growth, covered with small yellow flowers. The side shoots last one year, wither and are replaced by new 'tentacles'. The plant in its entirety is 10 cm. (4 in.) high.
Use: Rewarding indoor plant, even in a dry centrally heated atmosphere.
Soil: Soilless mixture or cactus soil (see p. 194) with good drainage. Deep pots on account of the long roots.
Feeding: 3 grams of fertiliser per litre (1 oz. per gallon) of water every 3 weeks (April–June).
Water: Moderate with complete drying out between each watering. Winter, very little water. Avoid applying water directly on to the plant.
Light: A lot of light, preferably full sunlight.
Heat: Summer, normal temperature. Winter, not below minimum 15°C. (60°F.).
Air: Dry room air.
Re-potting: February.
Propagation: By cuttings into plain sand.

Euphorbia canariensis

Habitat: Canary Islands.
Growth: Columnar, thorny stems, whi only branch at ground level.
Use and culture: As for *Euphorbia pu niformis.*

Euphorbia erythraea

Growth: High, candelabra-like, thor stems, covered with small, green folia leaves, which are shed during growth.
Use and culture: As for *Euphorbi pugniformis.* Will stand temperatures minimum 18–20°C. (65–70°F.) winter.

Euphorbia obesa

Habitat: South Africa, where the pl. is protected.
Growth: Globular stems, with d ridges which give the plant the appe ance of a fossilised sea urchin.
Use and culture: As for *Euphor pugniformis.* Easy to propagate fr seeds.

Euphorbia ramipressa

Growth: Flat, antler-like stems. quires a large amount of space brea wise.
Use and culture: As for *Euphorbia niformis.*

Euonymus japonicus

NOTE: Bleeding from wounds in lacerated stems can be stopped by squirting with warm water.

Euphorbia schimperi

Growth: Slender, smooth, succulent stems, almost without foliage leaves.
Use and culture: As for *Euphorbia igniformis*. Requires the minimum of attention.

Euphorbia undulatifolia

Growth: Stubby, round, smooth stems and oleander-like, hanging leaves.
Use and culture: As for *Euphorbia pugniformis*.

Celastraceae

Euonymus japonicus

Habitat: Japan.
Growth: Evergreen bush with coriaceous, green leaves and unattractive white flowers in great profusion. Varieties can be found with leaves variegated with yellow or white.
Use: Tub plant for conservatories and verandas. Can be left out of doors in the summer, but only in a warm spot.
Soil: Heavy, nourishing garden soil with bonemeal added as basic fertiliser.
Feeding: 5 grams of fertiliser per litre (¾ oz. per gallon) of water every 2 weeks (April–August).
Water: Summer, plenty; winter, moderate amounts, but the soil must not be allowed to dry out completely.
Light: Full or half-shade.
Heat: Normal temperature. Winter, protected from frost, but preferably at a minimum 5° C. (40° F.).
Air: Summer, damp air; winter, dry.
Repotting: Every other spring in tubs which are not too small.
Cutting: Trim back young shoots in order to form the plant.
Propagation: By cuttings of mature shoots in the spring.

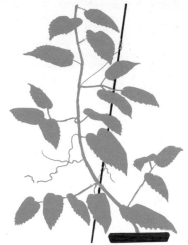

Cissus antarctica

Pests: Mealy bugs, scale insects.
Diseases: Mildew if exposed to too much dampness in winter.

Vitaceae

Cissus antarctica

Kangaroo Vine

Habitat: Australia.
Growth: Vigorous climbing plant, with shiny, oval, serrated leaves.
Use: Shade-plant for windows facing north, or possibly east or west, as long as there is not direct sunlight.
Soil: Light garden soil mixed with sand without peat.
Feeding: 4 grams of fertiliser per litre (1¼ oz. per gallon) of water every week (March–August). Never feed during the dark season.
Water: Moderate amounts. Sensitive to too much moisture, especially in winter.
Light: Slight shade; never direct sunlight.
Heat: Cool spot; winter best at minimum 15° C. (60° F.). Never place above a radiator.

Air: Normal room air.
Re-potting: Every year in February.
Cutting: Stopping young shoots fosters the development of side shoots.
Propagation: By cuttings in April–May.
Diseases: Brown spots on leaves are the result of too much light or moisture.
Other species: See below.

Cissus discolor

Habitat: Java.
Growth: Hanging shoots with attractive heart-shaped, olive-green leaves; these have silvery-grey marbling, and red undersides. The young leaves are violet-purple.
Use and culture: Hanging-bowl plant, which requires high temperature and very humid air. Only suitable for warm conservatories. Otherwise, the same as for *Cissus antarctica*.

Cissus striata

Habitat: Japan.
Growth: Richly branching, climbing plant with small, 5-fingered leaves.
Use and culture: Hanging-bowl or trellis plant in slightly shaded windows at normal room temperature. Otherwise, the same as for *Cissus antarctica*.

Cissus striata

Parthenocissus henryana

Habitat: China.
Growth: Deciduous climbing plant w metre-long (3-ft.) shoots. The leaves moss-green with silvery-white veins reddish-violet undersides.
Use: Suitable as a climbing plant w the trails tied to a small wire or bamb trellis, or as a hanging-bowl plant v trails hanging freely.
Soil: Soilless mixture.
Feeding: 4 grams of fertiliser per 1 ($\frac{1}{4}$ oz. per gallon) of water every w (April–July).
Water; Give enough but in moder amounts. Winter, relatively dry.
Light: Half-shade.
Heat: Temperatures should not be high. Winter, around minimum 8 (45° F.).
Air: Dry air.
Re-potting: February.
Cutting: Prune hard on re-potting.
Propagation: By cuttings of ma wood in February.
NOTE: No leaves during the 6-mo winter season.

Cissus discolor

hoicissus rhomboidea

atal Vine

abitat: South Africa.
rowth: Vigorous climbing plant with
foliate, glistening green leaves, the
dersides of which are covered with
own down.
se and culture: Suitable for a half-dark
om or for a window facing north. Re-
ires a lot of space. A more rewarding
door plant than *Cissus antarctica.*
lture otherwise the same.
rieties: 'Jubilee', with larger, coria-
ous leaves and slower growth. Very
ng-lasting indoors.

trastigma voinierianum

abitat: Asia.
owth: Very vigorous, climbing plant
th large leaves, consisting of 5 leaflets,
ich are reminiscent of the foliage of a
rse chestnut tree. Trails and young
ves are covered with reddish-brown
wn.
e: Trellis plant requiring a large
ount of space. Good ornamental
nt for conservatories, halls, vesti-
es and stairways.
il: Soilless mixture.
eding: 5 grams of fertiliser per litre

Tetrastigma voinierianum

(1½ oz. per gallon) of water every week
(March–August).
Water: Plenty in summer, allowing the
soil to dry out in between times. Winter,
very dry.
Light: Half-shade, no direct sunlight.
Heat: Cool room; winter, minimum 10–
15° C. (50–60° F.).
Air: Dry indoor air. Spray during the
spring.
Re-potting: March, in pots which are
not too small.
Tying up: Plenty of space between the
trails, so that the large leaves have
freedom to develop.
Propagation: By cuttings in February.
Pests: Red spider mites, mealy bugs.
Diseases: Yellow leaves with too little
nourishment.

Crassulaceae

Aeonium arboreum

Habitat: Canary Islands.
Growth: Trunked, branching succulent
with flat leaf rosette.
Use: May be cultivated in a sunny
window along with cacti, euphorbias
and other succulents. May be left out of
doors for the summer if in a warm spot.

Rhoicissus rhomboidea

Aeonium arboreum

Soil: Soilless mixture, with good drainage.
Feeding: 2 grams of fertiliser per litre ($\frac{1}{2}$ oz. per gallon) of water every 2 weeks (April–August).
Water: Summer, normal watering; winter, completely dry.
Light: Full sunlight.
Heat: Normal temperature; winter minimum 8° C. (46° F.).
Air: Dry indoor air.
Re-potting: Seldom necessary.
Propagating: By cuttings of side shoots in the spring.
Diseases: Rot and mildew can be caused by too much moisture in winter.
Variant: foliis-purpureis, with purple leaves.
Other species: See below.

Aeonium tabuliforme

Growth: Flat, plate-like rosette with dense leaves.
Use and culture: As for *Aeonium arboreum.*

Bryophyllum daigremontianum (87)

Habitat: Madagascar.
Growth: Succulent with oblong-pointed leaves with brown spots. In the inner

indentations of the leaf edge, numerou plantlets develop in the form of sma rosettes with fine roots. These sma plants are subsequently released and fa to the ground, where they immediatel strike roots. Pink flowers on a 30-cm (12-in.)-high stem.
Use: Good indoor plant for light wir dows.
Soil: Soilless mixture.
Feeding: 3 grams of fertiliser per lit (1 oz. per gallon) every 3 weeks (May August).
Water: Summer, normal watering; wi ter, almost dry.
Light: Sunlight.
Heat: Normal temperature; winter, be at minimum 12° C. (55° F.).
Air: Dry air.
Re-potting: Has a tendency to for long, leggy plants, thus rejuvenation growing on the plantlets is worth while
Propagation: By potting plantlets on they have fallen, in soil mixed with sar
Pests: Slugs and snails.
Other species: See below.

Bryophyllum tubiflorum (8

Growth: Thick, rod-shaped leaves w plantlets at their tips. The structure somewhat like that of a horsetail o conifer. The leaves are grey-green w

Cotyledon undulata

Crassula lactea

rker spots, the flowers orange-yellow
colour.
e and culture: As for *Bryophyllum
igremontianum.*

otyledon undulata

bitat: South Africa.
owth: Trunked succulent with thick,
ite-bloomed leaves with wavy edges.
rge clusters of orange-yellow tubular
wers in spring and summer.
e: Best in a sunny window.
il: Soilless mixture.
eding: 2 grams per litre ($\frac{1}{2}$ oz. per
lon) of water every 4 weeks (April–
y).
ater: Summer, normal, but not too
en. Winter, dry.
ht: Sunlight.
at: Summer, normal room tempera-
e; winter, best at minimum 12° C.
° F.).
: Dry air.
potting: By cuttings of tip growths.
uld be replaced from time to time,
ce old plants lose their bottom leaves.

assula portulacea   (89)

e Plant

bitat: South Africa.
owth: Small tree-like succulent with a
k trunk and numerous branches.
ck, roundish leaves. White starry
wers in great profusion early in spring.

Use: Best in a window facing south.
Soil: Soilless mixture.
Feeding: 3 grams of fertiliser per litre
(1 oz. per gallon) of water every 4 weeks
(April–July).
Water: Summer, only when the plant is
beginning to dry up completely. Winter,
dry.
Light: Sunlight.
Heat: Normal temperature; winter,
minimum 8° C. (45° F.).
Air: Dry air.
Re-potting: Seldom necessary.
Propagation: By cuttings in the spring.
Other species: See below.

Crassula falcata   (90)

Growth: The thick, felted leaves are
twisted and opposite, looking like ship's
propellers. Deep red flowers in the early
spring, in large, long-lasting inflorescences which grow so heavy that they
have to be supported.
Use and culture: As for *Crassula portulacea.*

Crassula lactea

Growth: Small succulent with thick,
blue-bloomed leaves. Small white starry
flowers in an open inflorescence.
Use and culture: As for *Crassula portulacea.*

Crassula lycopodioides

Growth: Flimsy plant with thin upright
shoots, the scaled leaves arranged in a

Crassula lycopodioides

regular pattern like the links in a zip fastener. White flowers.
Use and culture: As for *Crassula portulacea.*

Echeveria gibbiflora metallica (91)

Habitat: Mexico.
Growth: Large rosette of pretty, thick leaves with a metallic bronze sheen. The flowers are orange-red in spiked inflorescences. Long flowering period in the early spring.
Use: Best in windows facing south in full sunlight.
Culture: As for *Cotyledon undulata.*
Other species: See below.

Echeveria elegans (92)

Growth: Blue-bloomed rosette. Yellowy-white flowers in small clusters.
Use and culture: As for *Echeveria gibbiflora metallica.* Previously used for carpet bedding in gardens.

Kalanchoe blossfeldiana (93)

Habitat: Madagascar.
Growth: Compact plant with long-lasting, bright red flowers in thick tufts. The flowers on the dwarf varieties close up in the evening, while those of the taller varieties remain open day and night. Short-day plant which can be made to flower all year round by keeping in darkness for 14 hours out of 24 for 4 weeks.
Use: Attractive and very long-flowering ornamental plant.
Soil: Soilless mixture.
Feeding: 3 grams of fertiliser per litre (1 oz. per gallon) of water every 2 weeks (May–August).
Water: Summer, normal watering; more sparing in autumn and winter.
Light: Light or half-shade. The flowers are brightest in full sunlight.
Heat: Summer, normal temperature; winter, not below minimum 15° (60° F.).
Air: Will stand dry air.
Re-potting: After flowering has cease in pots which are not too large.
Cutting: Remove tops which ha ceased to flower, for the sake of the co tinued development of the plant.
Propagation: By cuttings or seed.

Rochea coccinea

Habitat: South Africa, where the pla is protected.
Growth: Upright stems, with der leaves arranged opposite one anoth and an umbel of crimson star flowers.
Use: Long-lasting, decorative sun pla with a powerful colour effect.
Soil: Soilless mixture.
Feeding: 3 grams of fertiliser per li (1 oz. per gallon) of water every 2 wee (March–July).
Water: Summer, normal; winter, dry.
Light: Sunlight.
Heat: Normal indoor temperature; w ter, minimum 8° C. (45° F.).
Air: Dry air.
Re-potting: February, in pots which not too large.
Cutting: Cut back to 15 cm. (6 above the ground after flowering ceased in June.
Propagation: By cuttings of s growths or by seed.

Rochea coccinea

iseases: Spots on leaves if too damp
during the winter.

axifragaceae

ydrangea macrophylla

abitat: Japan.
rowth: Vigorous bush, with brownish
anches, inverted oval leaves and large,
ll-shaped inflorescences, bearing
loured well-developed sepals and
herwise sterile flowers.
se: Ornamental plant for large-scale
rangement in a conservatory. With
ht covering, can be left to winter out
doors in a warm growth location.
il· Soilless mixture or acid soil,
4 5.5.
eding: 5 grams of fertiliser per litre
oz. per gallon) of water every week,
m 6 weeks after re-potting until the
ginning of August.
ater: Heavy consumption. Water
ice on hot days. More sparingly in
tumn and winter.
ght: No direct sunlight during flower-
. Otherwise, a light growth spot.
at: Frost-free winter, possibly in a
lar; after that, normal indoor tem-
ature.
: Humid air with spraying during
d after flowering.
potting: After flowering has ceased,
oot in spacious pots and at the same
e trim back the shoots which have
n in bloom. The newly developed
ots will flower the following year.
pagation: By cuttings in March.
ts: Greenfly, thrips.
rcing: Put in for forcing in January at
imum 15°C. (60°F.). Flowering
occur March–April at minimum
°C. (65°F.). Remember to water
erously, keep gently shaded and
ay. After flowering has ceased in
y, cut away the shoots which have
n in bloom. Growth period is June–
, with plenty of nourishment and
er. Resting period is August–

Hydrangea macrophylla

September, with moderate watering;
light and cool growth location, but pro
tect from frost.

Saxifraga stolonifera (94)
Mother of Thousands

Habitat: China and Japan.
Growth: Hanging plant with round, light-
veined leaves having red undersides,
gathered into rosettes. A 'beard' of red,
wiry runners with new, small rosettes
hangs down. White or light red flowers
in upright inflorescences, May–August.
Use: Attractive, undemanding hanging-
bowl plant.
Soil: Soilless mixture with good drain
age.
Feeding: 3 grams of fertiliser per litre
(1 oz. per gallon) of water every 2 weeks
(March–September).
Water: Evenly moist from March until
flowering has ceased in September.
After that, keep quite dry.
Light: Very light spot near a window,
otherwise the red leaves become discoloured.
Heat: Summer, normal temperature;
winter, minimum 12–15°C. (55–
60°F.).
Air: Dry indoor air.
Re-potting: Early spring in pots which
are not too large but with good drainage.

Tolmiea menziesii

Propagation: By taking plantlets from the ends of the runners.
Pests: Greenfly.

Tolmiea menziesii

Pick-a-back plant

Habitat: North America.
Growth: Luxuriant green plant with downy leaves on stems. New plantlets are formed at the base of the leaves. By putting a leaf into water or planting it in damp sand, roots develop rapidly on the tiny plant. Runners with miniature plants striking roots are also formed.
Use: Very easily satisfied plant even in unfavourable conditions in dense shade. May be used as a hanging-bowl plant with the runners hanging down. Can be left to winter out of doors in mild winters, like a good virtually evergreen ground plant in the shade of other plants.
Soil: Soilless mixture, pH 7.
Feeding: 2 grams of fertiliser per litre ($\frac{1}{2}$ oz. per gallon) of water every week in the light season.
Water: Plenty; must never be allowed to dry out completely.
Light: Can manage with very little light, e.g. in shaded windows facing north, halls or stairways.
Heat: Normal room temperature. Will stand temperatures near freezing point.
Air: Dry indoor air.

Re-potting: Spring, when the roots ha▪ filled the pot.
Propagation: By leaf cuttings, whic develop small plants at their base t▪ whole year round, or by division ▪ older plants in the spring.
Pests: Earwigs.
Variant: minima, which has sm▪ leaves, and is very profuse in its produ▪ tion of plantlets.

Pittosporaceae

Pittosporum tobira   (9

Habitat: China and Japan.
Growth: Evergreen bush with rhodode▪ dron-like leaves which are broad▪ towards the tip. Dense umbels of wh▪ flowers have an orange-blossom fr▪ rance.
Use: Tub plant for conservatories, t▪ races or patios. Cool winter in a fro▪ free cold greenhouse or conservatory.
Soil: Nourishing garden soil with ba▪ fertiliser added in the form of bonem▪ (Animix) and Peraform.
Feeding: 5 grams of fertiliser per li▪ ($1\frac{1}{2}$ oz. per gallon) of water every w▪ during the growth period.
Water: Summer, plenty; winter, j▪ enough to prevent the soil ball from d▪ ing out completely.
Light: Slight shade. Light winter.
Heat: Summer, normal temperatu▪ winter, minimum 5°C. (40°F.).
Air: Spraying in the spring.
Re-potting: Only occasionally.
Propagation: By seeding or cuttings.
Pests: Greenfly, scale insects.
Other species: See below.

Pittosporum undulatum

Growth: Dark, shiny leaves with slig▪ wavy edge. Somewhat reminiscent of leaves of the coffee tree.
Use and culture: As for *Pittospor▪ tobira*.

Eriobotria japonica

...saceae

...iobotria japonica

...quat

...bitat: China and Japan.

...wth: Vigorous bush with 25-cm.
-in.)-long, elliptical leaves; these
e attractive patterns on the upper
..., a brown felted appearance on the
...erside. The flat, fragrant flowers are
...hered into large clusters. Large
...m-like, yellow fruit with a delicate
...e.

...: Tub plant for large-scale arrange-
...ts, for example a cool conservatory
...veranda. Summer, out of doors in a
...m spot.

...l: Nourishing garden soil with bone-
...l added. Good drainage.

...ding: 5 grams of fertiliser per litre
...oz. per gallon) of water every week
...ing the growth period.

...ter: Summer, plenty; winter, dry.

...ht: Full sunlight.

...t: Summer, warm; winter, minimum
...C. (40° F.).

... Spray in spring.

...otting: Occasionally in deep tubs.

...pagation: By seed.

...s: Greenfly, scale insects.

Rosa hybrids (96)

Growth: Densely branching, thorny
bush with shiny, pinnate leaves and
double flowers in many colours with and
without fragrance.

Use: Ornamental plant, which is forced
into flowering in winter or spring. Resting period in autumn in a cool spot. The
types with dwarf-like growth and small
flowers are to be preferred as indoor
roses.

Soil: Soilless mixture or garden soil,
with a high content of clay and sand,
pH 6·5.

Feeding: 3 grams of fertiliser per litre of
water (1 oz. per gallon) every week
(February—August).

Water: Summer, normal watering; winter, moderate quantities, but do not
allow the soil to dry out completely.

Light: Light and sunny position, possibly out of doors.

Heat: Autumn and winter, cool
(minimum 5°C. (40° F.)). From
January onwards, slowly rising to minimum 15°C. (60° F.).

Air: Damp air with spraying during
forcing.

Re-potting: January, in deep pots. In the
greenhouse the pots should be plunged
in soil.

Cutting: Blooms which have finished
flowering are cut away to leave 2 green
leaves. Before commencement of
forcing, cut out weak shoots and prune
the remaining ones moderately.

Propagation: By cuttings in the spring,
or by budding in the late summer.

Pests: Greenfly, rose beetle.

Diseases: Mildew, black spot.

Varieties: Miniature rose varieties, *Rosa
chinensis minima*, which are 20–30 cm.
(8–12 in.) tall, are to be preferred for
indoor culture: 'Baby Masquerade'
(light yellow/rose red), 'Colibri'
(apricot-yellow/orange), 'Perle de
Montserrat' (pale pink/pearl white) and
'Zwergkönig' (crimson).

NOTE: Forcing for several years in

221

succession may be difficult, which is why new plants should be potted. It is not advisable to move flowering plants.

Leguminosae

Cytisus canariensis (97)

Genista

Habitat: Canary Islands.
Growth: Silk-down-covered shoots, and finely divided leaves. Clusters of yellow 'pea flowers' from February to May.
Use: Ornamental plant in the spring.
Soil: Soilless mixture or loam with peat added, pH 6·5.
Feeding: 3 grams of fertiliser per litre (1 oz. per gallon) of water every week from January until flowering. After flowering has ceased, re-potting should be done, then further application of fertiliser in the same doses until the end of August.
Water: From January to August, normal watering without drying out. Moderate watering after this.
Light: Likes full sunlight.
Heat: Summer, normal temperature, possibly out of doors. Autumn and winter, light and cool, but frost-free (minimum 5° C. (40° F.)) in December–January assists the development of buds). Subsequently, gradually warmer, up to 15° C. (60° F.) during flowering. If the plant is kept warmer than 15° C. (60° F.), flowering will not take place.
Air: Spray before and during flowering, otherwise dry air.
Re-potting: After flowering has ceased in deep, but not too spacious pots. Plant firmly, and avoid drying out.
Cutting: Plant may be shaped by stopping the summer shoots.
Propagation: By cuttings.
Other species: See below.

Cytisus × racemosus

Madeira Broom

Growth: Longer shoots with relatively dense down covering, and somewhat

earlier flowering than *Cytisus canaensis.* Use and cultivate otherwise in th same way. Has long-lasting, yello flowers.

Acacia cyanophylla (9

Habitat: Australia.
Growth: Elegant, thorny bush wi entire 'leaves', which are expanded le stems—or phyllodes—in contrast wi other *Acacia* species which have ve finely divided, mimosa-like leaves. profusion of yellow flowers in stemme round globe-like inflorescences.
Use: Good indoor plant for light, c conditions. Best in windows facing ea west or north, or in light conservatorie
Soil: Soilless mixture, or light san loam with clay and compost mixed in
Feeding: 2 grams of fertiliser per li (½ oz. per gallon) of water every 2 wee (April–July).
Water: The pot soil must always moist, but must not be under water or allowed to dry out completely. Go drainage is essential. Never have wa in the base dish.
Light: Slight shade.
Heat: Summer, normal temperat possibly outside in the sun and sh tered. Winter, minimum 8° C. (45° F.
Air: Will stand dry indoor air. Spra the spring.
Re-potting: At yearly intervals a flowering has ceased in May.
Propagation: By cuttings or seed.
Pests: Mealy bugs, scale insects.
NOTE: Take care to water properly.
Other species: See below.

Acacia dealbata decurrens (

Mimosa

Growth: Finely divided leaves. Glo shaped, yellow flowers are delightf fragrant, almost like foam rubber appearance.
Use: Imported early in spring as flowering branches from the Rivi

hich are sold under the name of
imosa. Not suitable for indoor culture
cept in large conservatories.

lbizzia lophantha

abitat: Australia.
owth: First-year plants have a single
ain stem, older plants are frequently
ore ramified. The leaves are bipannate,
d very decorative. The flowers grow
om pale yellow, cylindrical inflores-
nces.
e: Best in cool rooms or conserva-
ies. Summer, out of doors on a bal
ny or terrace. One-year plants are
st for indoor culture.
il: Soilless mixture.
eding: 2 grams of fertiliser per litre
oz. per gallon) of water every 2 weeks
pril–August).
ter: Evenly damp. Never allow
dry out completely, or to stand in
ter.
ht: Sunlight.
at: Summer, normal temperature;
ater, minimum 2° C. (36° F.).
: Damp, not enclosed.
potting: By seeds, which are sown at
igh temperature in January.

thrina crista-galli

oster-claw

bitat: Brazil.
wth: Sub-shrub with 3-fingered
es and colourful, coral red flowers
60-cm. (24-in.)-long inflorescences.
wering period, August–September.
: Tub plant for conservatories or
e windows facing south. Summer, on
rrace or in a flower room.
: Soilless mixture.
ding: 3 grams of fertiliser per litre
z. per gallon) of water every 2 weeks
ril–August).
er: Summer, plenty. Never allow to
out. Completely dry in winter.
it: Full light and sunny spot.

Lotus berthelotii

Heat: Summer, normal temperature.
From October to April, best at mini-
mum 5° C. (40° F.).
Air: Summer, fresh air; winter, com-
pletely dry.
Re-potting: April.
Propagation: By seed; should be sown
with bottom heat in January.

Lotus berthelotii

Habitat: Teneriffe.
Growth: Herbaceous perennial with
creeping and hanging stems covered
with silver down, and finely divided
leaves. The large scarlet flowers, shaped
like a bird's beak, appear in the early
spring.
Use: Hanging-basket plant for a sunny
window or conservatory. Winter, resting
period, during which the top withers
away.
Soil: Soilless mixture.
Feeding: 2 grams of fertiliser per litre
($\frac{1}{2}$ oz. per gallon) of water every week
during the growth period.

223

Water: Spring and summer, plenty of water. When drying out, all leaves are shed. Winter, fairly dry.
Light: Sunny growth spot.
Heat: Normal room temperature, but very cool though absolutely frost-free in winter.
Air: Spraying.
Re-potting: August.
Propagation: By seed or cuttings of young shoots in spring.

Mimosa pudica

Sensitive Plant

Habitat: Brazil.
Growth: Branching bush with feather-cut, sensitive leaves which fold up or hang down limply when touched, in strong winds or when exposed to sharp fluctuations in temperature. When the stimulus is withdrawn, the leaves and stems become distended with sap once more. When in darkness the leaves fold up in a sleeping position and do not react to being touched. The small, red-dish-mauve flowers are gathered into globe-shaped inflorescence.
Use: Interesting but not particular' durable indoor plant. Rejuvenation half-withered plants by cutting back not possible, therefore it must be cul' vated as an annual.
Soil: Soilless mixture.
Feeding: 2 grams of fertiliser per lit ($\frac{1}{2}$ oz. per gallon) of water every 2 wee (April–August).
Water: Normal watering the who year round. In spring and summer, t' soil must not dry out between wat ings.
Light: Half-shade or sunshine.
Heat: In growth period, over minimu $18°$C. ($65°$F.); in winter, somewh cooler (minimum $15°$C. ($60°$F.)).
Air: Very damp air in spring and su mer, otherwise normal indoor air.
Re-potting: February. Older, unattra tive plants should be discarded in favc of new 1-year plants.
Cutting back: Small plants can stopped at the 4th or 6th leaf, in order produce better branching.
Propagation: By seeds, which can sown several at a time to each pot, o' minimum $15°$C. ($60°$F.) in Februar March.

Onagraceae

Fuchsia hybrida (1(

Habitat: Tropical America.
Growth: Small, deciduous bush w hanging, lantern-like flowers in m colour combinations, especially wh pink, mauve, red and violet. There also double varieties.
Use: Easy indoor plant in light, but too warm, windows or conservator Summer, on a balcony or terrace. O' specimens can be cultivated as bus or standard tub plants.
Soil: Soilless mixture.
Feeding: 3 grams of fertiliser per l (1 oz. per gallon) of water every w

Mimosa pudica

March–September). Flowering will be
eagre if insufficient nourishment is
ven.
ater: Evenly damp soil; must not dry
it completely. Winter, very dry.
ight: Half shade. Winter, light.
eat: Normal temperature in summer;
nter, best at minimum 10° C. (50° F.).
ir: Damp air, with frequent spraying.
-potting: February.
utting: Cut back branches on re-
tting in the spring. Trunked plants are
rmed by tying up a single growth to a
mboo cane. All side shoots from the
ound and up along the trunk should be
moved, and the main stem stopped at
full height, from which the branches
ll radiate.
opagation: By cuttings in the spring.
sts: Greenfly.
rieties: Very many varieties, among
ich some are suitable for hanging-
wls, some for balcony boxes and
ne for use as pot plants.
TE: Very dry and cool winter. Re-
mber to remove withered leaves so
t nourishment is not used for fruit
aring. The fruit is, however, edible.

nicaceae

nica granatum   (101)

megranate

bitat: Mediterranean region.
owth: Up to 2 m. (6 ft.) in height.
ht green bush with small, shiny
ves positioned in pairs on red stems.
sturdy, garnet-red flowers grow 3
3 on strong dwarf-shoots. Varieties
to be found with white, yellow, pale
k and 2-colour-striped flowers; there
also double forms. The dwarf-form,
ch is normally used in indoor cul-
, flowers from its second year of life,
the main type does not flower until
r. The fruit seldom ripens in a British
mer.
The main type is used as a tub

plant in a conservatory and, in summer,
on a warm terrace or in an outside
room. The dwarf form is a rewarding
indoor plant.
Soil: Soilless mixture.
Feeding: 3 grams per litre of water
(1 oz. per gallon) every 2 weeks
(March–August).
Water: Plenty during summer, without
allowing constant dampness; drier from
March to October.
Light: Full sunlight.
Heat: Normal temperature in summer in
an airy window, or possibly out of
doors. Winter, minimum 8° C. (45° F.).
Air: Spray during the spring and summer, otherwise dry air.
Re-potting: February.
Cutting: Nip small shoots when re-pot-
ting: this produces a better crown form.
Propagation: By cuttings over high bot-
tom heat.
Variant: P.g. 'nana', 50 cm. (20 in.)
high. This dwarf form is better suited to
indoor culture than the main type.
Otherwise the same cultivation requirements.

Myrtaceae

Eucalyptus globulus   (102)

Blue Gum

Habitat: Australia.
Growth: Rapid-growing, evergreen tree
with angular trunks or stems. On young
plants, the aromatic, oval, blue-bloomed
leaves are non petiolate—unstalked—
and opposite. Later, the narrow petiolate, half-moon-shaped, hanging adult
leaves appear. Planted in Southern
Europe as a means of drying up malaria
swamps, as the tree absorbs and evaporates large quantities of water.
Use: Young plants are ornamental
indoor plants. They quickly become too
big for ordinary windows, however.
Older plants are therefore best used in
halls, conservatories or on verandas.

Soil: Soilless mixture.

Feeding: Large appetite. 3 grams per litre (1 oz. per gallon) of water every week (February–October).

Water: A lot of water during growth period, with no drying out in between. When kept cool for the winter, give enough water to prevent the soil from drying out altogether.

Light: As much as possible. The blue colour of the leaves will fade if the plant is put in too shady a spot.

Heat: Summer, normal temperature; winter, minimum 8° C. (45° F.).

Air: Will stand dry, indoor air, as long as sufficient water is given.

Re-potting: Young plants are re-potted every year in February, older plants somewhat less frequently.

Cutting: Bushy plants are formed by nipping the top shoots at the right time.

Propagation: By seed.

Myrtus communis

Myrtle

Habitat: Mediterranean countries.

Growth: Evergreen bush, the branches of which are often used for bridal crowns or bouquets. The small, coriaceous, dark green leaves have an aro-

Dizygotheca elegantissima

matic fragrance and flavour. The flow are snow-white, positioned on sh stems in the axils. Flowering peri June–September.

Use: Undemanding indoor plant windows facing east or west.

Soil: Soilless mixture, with good dra age.

Feeding: 4 grams per litre (1¼ oz. gallon) of water, every week (Marc July).

Water: Carefully with rainwater some other calcium-free water. B constant dampness and complete dry out should be avoided.

Light: Light location away from dir sunlight. The plant should be turned quently, so that it can develop evenly all sides.

Heat: Normal room temperature; w ter, minimum 8° C. (45° F.).

Air: Dry room air.

Re-potting: February, in pots which not too large.

Cutting: The plant can be shaped pruning and stopping young shoots can be grown as a standard with globe-shaped crown. Flowering is duced if cut back too extensively.

Myrtus communis

ropagation: By grafting in early
spring.
Pests: Scale insects.

...raliaceae

...izygotheca elegantissima

...ider Plant

Habitat: New Caledonia.
Growth: Elegant leaf plant, 50 cm.
(20 in.) high. Narrow, fingered, reddish
...own leaves with jagged edges. Older
...ants have larger leaves and small
...eenish flowers. The flowering form
...es under the name *Dizygotheca*
...rchoveana.
...e: Best in a window facing east or
...st, or a warm conservatory. Lasts for
...any years indoors.
...il: Soilless mixture.
...eding: 3 grams per litre (1 oz. per
...lon) of water every two weeks (March–
...ptember). Never give nourishment to
...y soil balls.
...ater: Summer, normal watering; win-
..., more moderate.
...ght: Half shade; never direct sunlight.
...at: Normal room temperature. Win-
..., not below minimum 15° C. (60° F.).
...quires more heat than other members
...the *Araliaceae.*
...: Needs damp air with frequent
...aying.
...-potting: Every 2 or 3 years in
...bruary.
...opagation: By seed.
...ts: Red spider mites.
NOTE: Needs absolutely damp air.
...ung plants are difficult to acclimatise,
...older established plants may thrive
...many years in the same spot.

...tshedera lizei (103)

...owth: A cross between *Fatsia japon-
...moseri,* the Castor Oil tree, and
...dera helix hibernica, Irish Ivy.
...orous, half-climbing plant with
...bed, dark green leaves.

Use: Leaf plant for halls, conservatories
and large windows. Rapidly grows too
large for normal windows, but can be
cut back and thus adjusted to the space
available. Will stand an indoor atmosphere better than many *Araliaceae.*
Culture: As for *Dizygotheca
elegantissima,* but will stand wintering
at a cooler temperature (minimum
10° C. (50° F.)).
Cutting: To compensate for the plant's
naturally poor branching, cutting back
each year in February can be recommended.
Pests: Scale insects, red spider mites.

Fatsia japonica

Castor Oil Tree

Habitat: Japan.
Growth: Vigorous foliage plant with 5–
7-lobed leaves.
Use: Will last for many years at normal
room temperature, or in a cool conservatory.
Culture: As for *Dizygotheca
elegantissima,* but requires a lower temperature in winter (minimum 10° C.
(50° F.)).
Cutting: Cutting back in February will
give a better spread of branches.
Pests: Greenfly, scale insects, red spider
mites.
Variant: moseri.
NOTE: If a choice has to be made between the 3 Aralia types, remember that
Fatshedera is the easiest one to handle,
while *Dizygotheca* is the most ornamental.

Hedera canariensis (104)

Canary Island Ivy

Habitat: Canary Islands.
Growth: Climbing plant with suction
roots on its stems and large almost
undivided leaves.
Use: Trellis plant in shaded windows, on

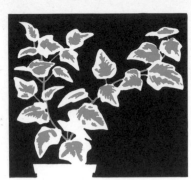

Hedera canariensis 'Variegata'

a wall, and as decoration for large rooms such as halls and vestibules. May also be used as a hanging-bowl plant, in rooms and conservatories.

Soil: Soilless mixture.

Feeding: 3 grams per litre (1 oz. per gallon) of water every week (April–September).

Water: Normal, but do not allow to dry out. Water more sparingly in the winter, however.

Light: Full or half-shade. At high room temperatures in the winter, give somewhat more light.

Heat: Does well in cool rooms.

Air: As humid as possible.

Re-potting: February, in pots which are not too large.

Cutting: Stopping young shoots may induce branching.

Tying up: The dwarf varieties are best used as hanging plants without tying up. Other types should be tied to wire or bamboo trellises. Sucks firmly on to quite smooth wall surfaces, from which the stems may later be difficult to remove.

Propagation: By grafting top shoots in August.

Pests: Scale insects, red spider mites.

Variants: 'Foliis variegatis' with ivory-blotched leaves.

Other species: See below.

Hedera helix (10.

Ivy

Habitat: Europe.

Growth: Well-known garden plan which also thrives indoors, even in po growth conditions.

Use and culture: As for *Hedera cana iensis.*

Variants: A few of the many ar *cavendishii*, with irregular, white le patterns; *crispa*, with small, friz leaves; *hibernica*, Irish ivy, which h very small leaves with fine, light n patterns; *ovata*, with almost hea shaped leaves; 'Pittsburgh', Star iv which has a very dense and compa growth, with short runners sending shoots from all axils, which is suitab for smaller windows; and *sagittaefol* Arrow-leaf ivy, with deeply indent almost arrow-shaped leaves.

Ericaceae

Erica gracilis (10

Christmas Heather

Habitat: South Africa.

Growth: Well-branched little bush, w tiny, fresh-green leaves and small, be shaped flowers in white, pink a purple. Flowers in late autumn and m winter.

Use: Long-lasting indoor flower in c conditions. In Germany it is used a seasonal plant for All Hallows Day, 1st November.

Soil: Peat, sand or garden soil with calcium content, pH 4.

Feeding: If the plant is in soil with low a nutrition content as peat, so fertiliser must be given, but the pl will not stand a high concentration salt in the soil, as this will scorch roots. So water carefully with 1 gram ordinary indoor plant fertiliser per l ($\frac{1}{4}$ oz. per gallon) every 2 weeks, al nating with 1 gram of urea per l

Hedera helix sagittaefolia

oz. per gallon), but only in May and ~~ne~~.

~~ater.~~ Plenty. If allowed to dry out ~~en~~ once, the plant may shed its leaves ~~d~~ wither. Remember also to keep the ~~il~~ moist in winter.

~~ght:~~ As well-lit a situation as possible. ~~ica~~ species are typical sun plants.

~~at:~~ Should spend the summer out of ~~ors.~~ Winter, minimum 10°C. ~~~°F.).~~

~~:~~ Spring and summer, humid air, ~~h~~ spraying. Drier in winter.

~~-potting:~~ After flowering has ceased ~~the~~ early spring, in pots which are not ~~~ large. Water thoroughly before re-~~cting.~~

~~tting:~~ Young shoots should be nipped ~~the~~ early spring, so as to produce ~~shy~~ plants. Nipping after 1st May ~~~duces poorer flowering.~~

~~pagation:~~ By cuttings in the spring.

~~TE:~~ The plant should be kept in a ~~~t~~ and cool—but frost-free— spot ~~~r~~ flowering has ceased.

~~er species:~~ See below.

~~ca~~ hiemalis

~~bitat:~~ South Africa.
~~wth:~~ Larger and more open than ~~ca~~ *gracilis*. Flowers in February–

March, with long, tube-like flowers in pale pink shades.
Use and culture: As above, but will not stand such extensive nipping, and not after 1st June.

Erica ventricosa

Habitat: South Africa.
Growth: Vigorous, dense growth with large, urn-shaped, light red or purple-red flowers gathered together at the end of the stems. Flowering period, May–July. Longer flowering if in a cool place.
Use and culture: As for *Erica gracilis*.

Erica wilmorei

Habitat: South Africa.
Growth: Upright growth, with very large, long tube-like flowers in shades of red. Flowering period, April–May.
Use and culture: As for *Erica gracilis*.

Rhododendron simsii   (107)

Indian Azalea

Habitat: Eastern Asia.
Growth: Small evergreen bush covered with brown down. The coriaceous leaves are dark green with lighter undersides, the flowers are both single and double, in white and all shades of red. Natural flowering in May, but now forced in nurseries commercially for sale from August to May.
Use: Colourful ornamental plant for autumn, winter and spring. Repeated flowering may present some difficulty with older plants under indoor culture.
Soil: Soilless mixture, or a special 'azalea soil' consisting of a mixture of peat, spruce or pine needles together with well-rotted horse manure. pH 4–4.5.
Feeding: 3 grams per litre (1 oz. per gallon) of water every week (March–August).
Water: Only use rainwater or some other soft water, possibly mains water

neutralised by 1 gram ammonium sulphate per litre ($\frac{1}{4}$ oz. per gallon). Water generously during flowering and growth, from the top and not into base dishes. Once a week the plant should be bathed by dipping the entire pot into lukewarm water, so that the soil ball is thoroughly wetted. If allowed to dry out even once, the plant is liable to shed its leaves and possibly wither away completely. During the development of buds in the early autumn, water generously.

Light: Full or half-shade. Flowering may cease too quickly in full sunlight.

Heat: Flowering lasts longer in a cool place. After flowering has ceased, the plant should be placed in a warm spot away from direct sunlight out of doors. In September it should be taken back indoors and placed in a light, cool spot (minimum 10°C. (50°F.)), until forcing begins in December.

Air: Damp air with spraying during the growth period.

Re-potting: Directly after flowering has ceased in May–June. Make sure the soil ball is thoroughly wet before re-potting.

Propagation: By cuttings or by grafting.

Diseases: Leaf shedding as a result of drought. Yellow leaves and shoot tips in soil containing calcium.

NOTE: Winter and spring: Flowering period with plenty of water, a lot of nourishment and a temperature of 15°C. (60°F.). Re-pot in May. May–August: Growth period with plenty of water, a lot of nourishment and a warm spot out of doors. September: Resting period and formation of buds, with moderate watering, no nourishment and a cool location (minimum 10°C. (50°F.)). Forcing, January–March.

Varieties: A large number of varieties in many colours and shapes.

Other species: See below.

Rhododendron obtusum

Growth: Not such compact growth as *Rhododendron simsii*, and smaller,

elegant flowers. Use and culture othe wise the same.

Primulaceae

Cyclamen persicum giganteum (10?

Cyclamen

Habitat: Middle East.

Growth: Tuberous plant with wid petiolate, heart-shaped leaves whi have attractive patterns. The flowers a lifted up over the foliage by succule smooth stems, and the petals, which a attractively swept back, may be found white and all shades of red. There a also types with semi-double flowers, a others with fringed petals. A good co mercial plant should have vigoro foliage with firm stems, upright flo stems and a large number of buds on t way up from the tuber.

Use: Outstanding and long-lasting or mental plant which is in season autumn, winter and spring.

Soil: Soilless mixture with good dra age.

Feeding: 3 grams of fertiliser per li (1 oz. per gallon) of water every week summer, every 2 weeks in winter, a always to a soil ball which is alrea moist.

Water: Plenty in summer; winter, required, without allowing to dry c The tuber itself and the flower buds o must not be wetted. Watering in a b dish is recommended. Superfluous w which has not been absorbed after an hour should be poured away.

Light: Full or half-shade. Light in w ter, but without direct sunlight.

Heat: November–February, minim 10°C. (50°F.); the rest of the ye minimum 15–18°C. (60–65°F.). warm rooms, incipient buds will develop and existing flowers will f quickly.

Air: Spray frequently in summer. In six months of the winter season, f October, the air should be kept dry.

Re-potting: After flowering has ceased in April–May. At the same time, remove old dry roots.
Propagation: By seed.
Pests: Greenfly, thrips.
NOTE: The plant should be maintained in growth the whole year round without a resting period. Cool and light in winter, cool and damp in summer. The soil ball should never be allowed to dry out completely. New leaves should develop before the old ones wither away.

Primula malacoides (109)

Fairy Primrose

Habitat: Yunnan province in China.
Growth: Annual herbaceous plant with rosette of long-stemmed oval leaves, and many whorls of small, stalked flowers in white, pink, mauve or red. The whole plant is more or less white-powdered.
Use: Ornamental plant in winter and spring. Can seldom be forced a second time.
Soil: Peat, with sandy soil and compost mixed in, possibly loamless compost. Good drainage.
Feeding: 1 gram of fertiliser per litre (oz. per gallon) of water every 2 weeks. The roots are scorched if there is too high a content of fertiliser salts in the soil.
Water: The soil ball must always be moist, but never water in the base dish. Dried out plants can be rescued by immersing the pot in a container with lukewarm water for a couple of hours.
Light: Half shade, never direct sun. The colour of the flowers will fade, however, if too little light is given.
Heat: Cool location. Winter, not more than minimum 10° C. (50° F.).
Air: Humid air.
Re-potting: The plant is usually discarded after flowering has ceased.
Cutting: Stems which have finished flowering are removed, to encourage

Primula obconica

new flower stems to form and extend the flowering period 3–4 months.
Propagation: By seed.
Other species: See below.

Primula obconica

Habitat: China.
Growth: Vigorous, perennial indoor primula, with long-stemmed, roundish, whole-edged leaves, and long flower stems bearing large balls of flat-collared flowers in white, pink, red and violet. Both leaves and stems are covered with gland hairs; these contain a substance which may cause dermatitis in susceptible people, and anyone allergic to this should wear gloves when handling the plants. In Germany, varieties containing practically no irritant are produced under the name *Nonprimina Bayernblut*.
Use: Rewarding ornamental plant for winter and spring.
Culture: As for *Primula malacoides*. But since the plant is a perennial, it must be re-potted after flowering has ceased in May, in pots which are not too large. The soil should be more sandy than the

Primula sinensis

mixture specified for the above type. After re-potting, the plant should be placed in a damp, semi-shaded location for the whole of the summer. Has no particular resting period.

Primula sinensis

Habitat: China.
Growth: Long-stemmed, segmented, downy leaves. Dense inflorescence, with large, flat-collared flowers on relatively short stems. Flower colours can be white, pink, red, blue and violet.
Use: Good indoor plant for cool, light windows.
Culture: As for *Primula obconica*. Re-potting after flowering has ceased. Sensitive to lingering moisture, which is why the pot must have good drainage. The root neck should be placed above the surface of the soil when re-potting, so that the plant almost rests upon the ground, supported by a couple of matches or small sticks. Planting too deeply will cause rot in the neck of the plant.

Primula kewensis (110)

Growth: A cross between the Primula species *floribunda* and *verticillata*
232

produced at Kew Gardens, in England Has longish, powdery leaves. A tal stem with whorls of short-stalked butter yellow flowers; indeed, the only indoo primula with yellow blossom.
Use: Annual ornamental plant for cool light windows.
Culture: As for *Primula malacoides* Difficult to cultivate for more than on season.

Plumbaginaceae

Plumbago capensis (11)

Plumbago

Habitat: South Africa.
Growth: Long, pendulous stems wit light green leaves, arranged spirally. Th light blue, phlox-like flowers are bor in large umbels, and the unusually lor flowering period extends from March November.
Use: Long-flowering indoor plant f light windows. Older plants require su porting or tying-up. Large plants tubs can be left out of doors for th summer.
Soil: Soilless mixture.
Feeding: 3 grams of fertiliser per lit (1 oz. per gallon) of water every we (March—November).
Water: Plenty. Drier from November February.
Light: As light as possible in sout facing window. The pot should be pr tected against drying out in direct su shine.
Heat: Most luxuriant flowering at hi temperatures. From November February, best at minimum 12° (55° F.). Must not be placed in a c lar. The roots should always be k cool.
Air: Dry indoor air.
Re-potting: February.
Cutting: Prune long shoots at the sa time as re-potting.
Propagation: By cuttings.

Polemoniaceae

Cobaea scandens (112)

Habitat: Mexico.

Growth: Rapidly-growing, perennial climbing plant, the tendrils of which support the stems together. Bell-shaped, violet flowers appear throughout the summer and autumn.

Use: Normally treated as an annual climbing plant for use indoors or out of doors on a trellis. Will survive the winter easily if protected from frost, and can be used as a perennial indoor plant for trellising in large windows and cool conservatories. A permanent trellis is unsuitable where the plant cannot spend the winter in the growth location, but must be moved to a cooler spot.

Soil: Soilless mixture.

Feeding: 2 grams per litre ($\frac{1}{2}$ oz. per gallon) of water every week (March–September).

Water: Plenty in summer; winter, dry.

Light: Flowers best in a light location.

Heat: Summer, normal temperature; winter, minimum 8° C. (46° F.).

Air: Ordinary indoor air.

Re-potting: Early spring, before forcing begins at normal room temperature.

Cutting: Extensive pruning at the time of re-potting. In addition, thin out the shoots a few times during the course of the summer in order to get air to the plant and to promote flowering.

Propagation: By seed.

Varieties: There is a white variant.

Convolvulaceae

Pharbitis tricolor (113)

Morning Glory

Habitat: Central America.

Growth: Vigorous, annual twining plant with a great profusion of large, heart-shaped leaves and red, violet or blue trumpet-shaped bindweed flowers, each of which only opens for a single day.

Use: Trellis plant for a large, bright window, conservatory or outdoor summer location free from wind.

Soil: Soilless mixture.

Feeding: 2 grams per litre ($\frac{1}{2}$ oz. per gallon) of water every week (April–September).

Water: Plenty.

Light: Sunlight.

Heat: Normal summer temperature.

Air: Spray during hot weather.

Re-potting: This is only an annual.

Tying-up: The stems must be spread out on the trellis at the start, so that they do not tangle.

Cutting: Removal of withered flowers assists further flowering.

Propagation: By seeding under glass in March.

Pests: Greenfly, red spider mites.

Varieties: 'Clark's Blue' (sky blue) and 'Scarlett O'Hara' (claret-coloured).

Boraginaceae

Heliotropium arborescens

Heliotrope

Habitat: Peru.

Growth: Evergreen sub-shrub with very dark green, veined leaves, and flat umbels of dark violet, delicately fragrant flowers in summer and autumn.

Heliotropium arborescens

Use: Ordinary plant for putting out in balcony-boxes, flower-bowls and garden-beds. Also suitable as a garden plant on the lines of *Geraniums* and *Busy Lizzie.*
Soil: Soilless mixture.
Feeding: 2 grams per litre ($\frac{1}{2}$ oz. per gallon) of water every week (May–August).
Water: Plenty.
Light: Bright window, but not exposed to scorching sunshine.
Heat: Summer, normal room temperature; winter, minimum 12° C. (55° F.).
Air: Spray frequently in hot weather.
Re-potting: Spring, before growth begins.
Cutting: Nip out the tops of the shoots in spring in order to shape the plant and to provide several flowering shoots.
Propagation: By cuttings in autumn and/or spring.

Solanaceae

Browallia speciosa

Habitat: Tropical America.
Growth: Sub-shrub, cultivated as an

Browallia speciosa

annual. The leaves are broad and lanc shaped. Blue, bell-shaped flowers, 4 cm ($1\frac{3}{4}$ in.) across; only a few appear simu taneously, but the plant has a lor flowering period.
Use: A non-permanent, undemandir indoor plant, which can be made flower at almost any season of the yea
Soil: Soilless mixture.
Feeding: 2 grams per litre ($\frac{1}{2}$ oz. p gallon) of water every 2 weeks (March August).
Water: Normal watering, but do n allow to dry out.
Light: Light or half-shade.
Heat: Normal, but not too high roc temperature.
Air: Spray in hot weather.
Re-potting: Retention over the win and re-potting are not worth while.
Cutting: Nip or cut back after m flowering period, as this will enable t plant to flower again.
Propagation: By seed.

Brunfelsia calycina   (1 l

Habitat: Brazil.
Growth: Small bush with coriaceo dark green leaves. Large, flat-collar violet flowers which, when flowering coming to an end, fade to a weak sh of pale blue. Normal flowering per from February to September; un good growth conditions, the whole y round.
Use: Easy, long-flowering indoor plar
Soil: Soilless mixture with good dr age.
Feeding: 3 grams per litre (1 oz. gallon) of water every 2 weeks (Mar September), but only apply to moist balls.
Water: Normal watering, but do allow lingering moisture during growth period. Sparingly during winter, but do not allow to dry out c pletely.
Light: Half-shade; winter, light.
Heat: Normal room temperature,

void major fluctuations. Winter, not
below minimum 15° C. (60° F.).
Air: Damp air with frequent spraying.
Re-potting: February in flat pots.
Cutting: Nip the top shoots of young
plants.
Propagation: By cuttings over minimum
30° C. (85° F.) bottom heat in spring.
Variants: eximea, with large, purple-
violet flowers, and *floribunda,* which
flowers most prolifically.
NOTE: In order to get air to the roots,
loosen the top soil at suitable intervals
or possibly top dress, but take care not
to damage the roots at the surface of the
soil.
Other species: See below.

Brunfelsia hopeana

Growth: Pale violet flowers in great
profusion.
Use and culture: As for *Brunfelsia
calycina,* but requires more heat. Sensitive to lingering moisture and drought,
best in a hothouse or heated conservatory.

Cestrum purpureum (115)

Habitat: Mexico.
Growth: Metre-high (3-ft.) bush with
overhanging branches, large full-edged
leaves and clusters of tubular purple
flowers from March to July.
Use: Space consuming, elegant plant for
large flower windows or conservatories.
Soil: Soilless mixture.
Feeding: 2 grams per litre ($\frac{1}{2}$ oz. per
gallon) of water every 2 weeks (March–
August).
Water: Plenty during the summer, very
dry in winter.
Light: Half-shade.
Heat: Normal temperature in summer;
winter, minimum 12° C. (55° F.).
Air: Normal indoor air.
Re-potting: Early spring, before the
growth period begins.
Cutting: Cut back when re-potting.

Propagation: By cuttings over high bottom heat.

Datura suaveolens (116)

Angel's Trumpet

Habitat: Mexico.
Growth: Sturdy bush with soft, slightly
downy leaves and large white, trombone-
like hanging flowers having their tips
curved backwards. Delicate fragrance.
Flowering period, June–November.
Use: Small plants for indoor use. Larger
plants are more suitable for tubs in halls
or conservatories, or on a sunny, shel-
tered terrace out of doors during the
summer.
Soil: Soilless mixture.
Feeding: 5 grams per litre ($1\frac{1}{2}$ oz. per
gallon) of water every week (February–
September). Large appetite.
Water: Plenty. Drought causes the
leaves to droop limply.
Light: Sunlight or half-shade. Light
location during the winter.
Heat: Summer, normal temperature;
winter, minimum 10° C. (50° F.).
Air: Will stand dry air. Avoid drops of
water on flowers, or moisture dripping
from trees out of doors in the summer.
Re-potting: February, in pots which are
not too large, or in tubs.
Cutting: The crown can be shaped by
light pruning in February. Standard
trees are developed by the removal of
side shoots on the stem up to the
required height.
Propagation: By cuttings in early
spring.
Pests: Red spider mites, snails and
slugs.
NOTE: The sap and seeds are *poisonous.*
Other species: See below.

Datura sanguinea

Growth: 20 cm. (8 in.) long, red and
yellowy-green funnel-shaped flowers in
autumn.

Use and culture: As for *Datura suaveolens*. No definite resting period.

Solanum capsicastrum (117)
Christmas Cherry

Habitat: Southern Brazil.
Growth: Small bush with narrow, shiny, lance-shaped leaves and white flowers in May. Round or oval fruits in shades of orange and red develop in the late summer.
Use: Easily satisfied indoor plant, decorative when bearing fruit.
Soil: Soilless mixture.
Feeding: 3 grams per litre (1 oz. per gallon) of water every 2 weeks (April–August).
Water: Summer, plenty; winter, moderate. No real resting period.
Light: Semi-shaded or light location. Sunshine needed for the attractive fruit colouring.
Heat: Normal room temperature during the flowering and fruit-bearing periods. After the fruit have fallen in winter, cooler (minimum 15° C. (60° F.)).
Air: Dry room air.
Re-potting: Early spring, well before flowering commences, but the plant is usually treated as an annual and discarded after bearing fruit.
Propagation: By seed.
Pests: Greenfly, thrips, red spider mites.
Other species: See below.

Solanum pseudocapsicum

Habitat: Madeira.
Growth: Produces slightly larger berries than *Solanum capsicastrum*. Use and culture otherwise the same.

Scrophulariaceae

Calceolaria herbeohybrida (118)
Slipper Flower

Habitat: Andes Mountains.
Growth: One-year herbaceous plant

Solanum pseudocapsicum

with succulent, green leaves and bright coloured, blown-out, spotted flowe with a mesh pattern.
Use: Ornamental plant, but only whi flowering in the spring. Short-lived.
Soil: Soilless mixture.
Feeding: Unnecessary, if the plants a bought already in flower and thrown o after flowering has ceased.
Water: Plenty of water, and do n allow to dry out. May need wateri several times a day in hot conditions.
Light: Light location away from dire sunshine.
Heat: As cool a spot as possible. T flowers last longest at minimum 1 12° C. (50–55° F.).
Air: Very damp air with frequent spr ing.
Re-potting: The plant is thrown out af flowering has ceased.
Propagation: Seeding in July–Augu Transplant one month later, and pot small pots in October. Maintain a c stant temperature of minimum 12° (55° F.), but in order to assist the velopment of flower buds, subject t 'cool treatment' at minimum 8 (47° F.) for a month as soon as the pl has acquired 5–6 green leaves. A that, revert to minimum 12° C. (55° also during the flowering period.
Pests: Slugs and snails.
Diseases: Grey mould.

Hebe andersonii

Habitat: New Zealand.

Growth: Small, evergreen bush with lance-shaped leaves and pale, violet-blue flowers in brush-like inflorescences, August–October.

Use: Chiefly an indoor foliage plant, but can also be used out of doors in the summer in balcony-boxes, tubs or in borders.

Soil: Soilless mixture.

Feeding: 3 grams per litre (1 oz. per gallon) of water every 2 weeks (April–August).

Water: Summer, normal watering, winter, very dry.

Light: Light and sunny location, especially in the winter.

Heat: Relatively cool. Winter, frost free, just at minimum 5° C. (40° F.).

Air: Dry indoor air.

Re-potting: February.

Propagation: By cuttings in spring.

Variant: 'Variegata', with white-edged, green leaves, which is the one most often cultivated.

Gesneriaceae

Achimenes coccinea

Habitat: Central America.

Growth: Cone-shaped stem tubers with upright, down-covered stems. The leaves are oval, serrated and down-covered; the plant has flat, plate-like, red flowers in the axils. Flowering period, June–October.

Use: Luxuriantly flowering indoor plant for windows facing east or west.

Soil: Soilless mixture.

Feeding: 3 grams per litre (1 oz. per gallon) of water every 2 weeks during growth period, until flowering commences.

Water: Keep the soil evenly moist from March to October. Always take the chill off the water, and avoid water dripping on to the leaves and flowers. Keep completely dry during the resting period, October–February.

Light: Half-shade.

Heat: Force in March–April at minimum 20–25° C. (70–80° F.). Afterwards, normal room temperature until October. Keep at minimum 10° C. (50° F.) during the winter.

Air: Slightly damp air during forcing in March–April, otherwise normal indoor air.

Re-potting: The tubers should be potted in February, 3–5 in each pot, covered with 2 cm. (1 in.) of soil. Further re-potting unnecessary.

Propagation: By division of tubers.

Pests: Greenfly.

NOTE: Keep to the October–February resting period with the temperature at a minimum 10° C. (50° F.) and completely dry.

Other species: See below.

Achimenes longiflora (119)

Growth: Plain blue flowers. Also types in white, pink, scarlet and light and dark blue.

Use and culture: As for *Achimenes coccinea.*

Aeschynanthus lobbianus

Habitat: East Indies.

Growth: In nature, an epiphyte on tree

Hebe andersonii

Aeschynanthus lobbianus

trunks. Hanging stems with thick, dark green leaves. The bright red flowers are mounted in a downy, tubular calyx with dark stripes.

Use: Can be used as a flowering plant in windows facing east or west, as a hanging plant, or as a ground plant in a conservatory.

Soil: Soilless mixture.

Feeding: 3 grams per litre (1 oz. per gallon) every 2 weeks (March–September).

Water: The plant is kept completely dry for the whole of May to allow the development of flower buds. Otherwise normal watering. Only use lukewarm water. Do not pour water directly on to leaves and flowers.

Light: Full or half-shade.

Heat: During the resting period in May, less than minimum 15°C. (60°F.), otherwise around minimum 20°C. (70°F.).

Air: Humid.

Re-potting: April.

Propagation: By cuttings of shoot tips

238

or by cuttings from stem pieces in earl spring.

Pests: Greenfly, red spider mites, snai and slugs.

Hypocyrta radicans (12(

Clog plant

Habitat: Brazil.

Growth: Upright or semi-hanging ster with thick, shiny oval leaves. The orang red flowers are tube-like, pressed togeth in front, with an orange-yellow ri Flowers in spring and summer.

Use: Ornamental flowering plant summer. Evergreen indoor plant outsi the flowering season.

Soil: Soilless mixture.

Feeding: 3 grams per litre (1 oz. gallon) of water every 2 weeks (Marc September). Only give nourishme when the soil ball is moist.

Water: Regular watering, witho allowing to dry out, but no lingeri moisture. Winter, more sparingly. O use tepid water.

Light: Shaded or semi-shaded locatio winter, lighter.

Heat: Summer, normal room tempe ture. Winter, minimum 15°C. (60°) but only minimum 12°C. (55°F.) d ing the 6 weeks in December–Janu when the buds are developing.

Air: Humid air.

Re-potting: February, in flat dishes.

Propagation: By top cuttings, which strike roots at minimum 25°C. (77° bottom heat.

Diseases: Ring markings appear leaves when the water used for water is too cold.

Pests: Greenfly.

Columnea hybrida (1

Habitat: Costa Rica.

Growth: Hanging plant with thin tr up to a metre (3 ft.) in length, den covered with small, opposite red leaves. The flowers are orange-red olour, and appear in the axils. From me to time, attractive red berries also ppear.

se: Good hanging-bowl plant in warm onditions, e.g. a conservatory.

oil: Soilless mixture.

eeding: 2 grams per litre ($\frac{1}{2}$ oz. per allon) of water, every week (January– eptember).

ater: Leave without water for the hole of December, the plant's resting riod, in order to assist the formation flower buds. After that, normal water- g with tepid water, but without allow- g to dry out, until September. More aringly in October and November, adually cutting down the amounts til the resting period. Additional wering can be obtained by adding a onth's extra rest at the height of the mmer, with no water or nourishment d in a cool location.

ght: Half-shade, never direct sunlight.

at: During the resting period in cember, minimum 10° C. (50° F.). ter that, minimum 20° C. (70° F.) for entire growth period until ptember. In autumn, minimum 15° C.)° F.). Avoid major fluctuations in ytime temperature.

: High degree of air humidity. Keep air damp, but do not spray directly to the leaves, which will cause brown ts to appear.

Episcia reptans

Re-potting: In pans, after flowering has ceased.

Propagation: By cuttings from stems, which are covered with soil.

NOTE: Do not forget constant temperature, no draughts and humid air.

Varieties: 'Vega', with orange-red, yellow-throated flowers, and 'Capella'.

Other species: See below.

Columnea microphylla

Growth: Elegant hanging plant with thin stems and very small, green, downy leaves. Orange-red flowers have yellow throats and yellow stripes on their corolla tubes.

Use and culture: As for *Columnea hybrida*. Needs warmth.

Episcia reptans

Habitat: Columbia and Brazil.

Growth: Creeping stems with runners, which carry small plants. Downy, olive green leaves with lighter veins and reddish undersides. Small, clear red flowers in the summer-time.

Use: Good hanging-bowl plant in slightly shaded location.

Soil: Soilless mixture with good drainage.

Feeding: 2 grams per litre ($\frac{1}{2}$ oz. per gallon) of water every 2 weeks (April– August).

Water: Regular watering. Will not stand either drying out or too much water.

Light: Window facing east or west.

Heat: Not less than 15° C. (60° F.) during growth period, March–September. Winter, minimum 10° C. (50° F.).

Air: High degree of air humidity, but do not water or spray directly on to the foliage. Will not stand draughts.

Re-potting: April, in flat dishes.

Propagation: By runners which have taken root. Older plants are less attractive and should be replaced by new ones every 2 years.

Kohleria eriantha

Pests: Red spider mites, thrips, snails and slugs, wood lice.
NOTE: Needs warmth, damp air and very light location.

Kohleria eriantha

Habitat: Central America.
Growth: Scale-like tubers. Oval, dark green leaves with red down. Bell-shaped flowers with a narrow tube and collar inclined outwards. The flowers, which are thickly covered with down, are orange-red with yellow spots on their inner sides.
Use: Good indoor plant in a warm, shaded flower window.
Soil: Soilless mixture.
Feeding: 3 grams per litre (1 oz. per gallon) of water every 3 weeks (April–August).
Water: Even watering the whole year round, but must not dry out. Always use water at room temperature.
Light: Shaded or semi-shaded location.
Heat: Summer, minimum 25°C. (77°F.); winter, not less than 12°C. (55°F.).
Air: Damp air.
Re-potting: March, in flat pots.
Propagation: By division of tubers.
Pests: Thrips.

Rechsteineria cardinalis

Habitat: South America.
Growth: Tuberous plant with very so velvet-green leaves covered with fi down. Long, tube-like scarlet flowe Flowering season, May–September.
Use: Best in warm, slightly shade flower windows, or possibly conserv tories.
Soil: Soilless mixture with good drai age.
Feeding: 2 grams per litre ($\frac{1}{2}$ oz. p gallon) of water every week fro the beginning of growth to flowerir Only give nourishment to damp s balls.
Water: Keep constantly damp in spri and summer. After flowering has ceas reduce watering gradually and st completely when the leaves and ste wither prior to the winter resting peric which lasts from November February.
Light: Full or half-shade.
Heat: Needs a lot of warmth. Summ minimum 25°C. (77°F.); autun minimum 20°C. (70°F.). The c tubers should be kept at minim 15°C. (60°F.) for the winter.

Rechsteineria cardinalis

ir: Very damp air. When spraying, use
arm water at minimum 25°C.
(7°F.).

e-potting: Tubers which have been
:pt dry for the winter ar taken out of
ie soil in February and replanted in
esh soil. When growth is vigorous, fur-
ier re-potting may be necessary during
e course of the summer.

ropagation: By division of large tubers
February.

iseases: Watering with water which is
o cold produces round, brown spots
i the leaves.

sts: Thrips (when the air is too dry
d the light too intense).

>TE: Always remember to keep the
bers warm and dry in the winter.

hmannia angulata

inese Foxglove

abitat: China.
owth: Perennial with rosettes of large,
iented, downy leaves. The flower
ms are about 40 cm. (16 in.) high,
d bear large purple trumpet-flowers
:h orange-yellow spots in their throats
May—July.
e: Ornamental plant for semi shaded
ations in cool rooms.
il: Soilless mixture.
eding: 2 grams per litre ($\frac{1}{2}$ oz. per
lon) of water every week in spring
I early summer.
ter: Keep evenly moist during
wth period, after which moderate
ounts of water.
ht: Half shade.
at: Cool, airy spot away from
ughts; summer, minimum 15°C.
°F.), winter, minimum 8°C.
°F.).
: Dry indoor air.
potting: Spring, before growth
ins. The top withers in the autumn,
vith all perennials.
pagation: By division in spring or by
ding.

NOTE: May be difficult to keep as a permanent indoor plant. Biennial culture
may therefore be preferable.

Saintpaulia ionantha   (122)

African Violet

Habitat: Usambara Mountains in
Kenya.
Growth: Rosette plant with thick, oval,
downy, petiolate leaves. The flowers are
gathered into small, loose clusters, 2—6
together, shaped rather like violets. The
original type has dark violet flowers
with bright yellow anthers. There are
varieties, both single and double, with
light-blue, white, mauve and pink
flowers.
Use: Rewarding, all-year flowering
indoor plant, for locations which are not
too cool.
Soil: Garden soil, with compost, leaf
mould and gravel added. Good drainage. Soilless mixture or other peat-
containing mixtures are not particularly
suitable.
Feeding: 3 grams per litre (1 oz. per
gallon) of water every 2 weeks, in water
with the chill taken off it, April—
September.
Water: The soil should always be moist,
but without retained water. As the plant
will not stand moisture being dripped on
to leaves and flowers, water into base
dishes and pour the excess water away
after half an hour. Only use warm water
at a minimum 25°C. (80°F.).
Light: Half-shade, but light during the
winter. Absolutely no direct sunlight.
Heat: Normal room temperature, but
not below minimum 15°C. (60°F.).
Air: Damp air. But avoid spraying,
which will produce ugly spots on the
leaves. Will not stand draughts.
Re-potting: Spring or early summer, in
flat pots.
Propagation: By leaf cuttings in spring.
Diseases: Mildew. Brown ring-marks on
the leaves are caused by using water
which is too cold.

Sinningia speciosa (123)

Gloxinia

Habitat: Brazil.

Growth: Tuberous plant with short stems which have large, shaggy, velvety, very brittle leaves. The large, bell-shaped flowers are white, red, red with white edges, or blue. Flowering period, May–October.

Use: Lasts longest in a flower window or conservatory with temperature and air humidity maintained at constant levels.

Soil: Equal amounts of peat, leaf mould and sand, possibly a compost mixture.

Feeding: 3 grams per litre (1 oz. per gallon) of water every week from February until flowering begins. No nourishment after that.

Water: Keep the soil evenly moist during the spring and summer, but do not allow to dry out. Use water at a minimum temperature of 25° C. (80° F.). When flowering has ceased in October, reduce the watering gradually, and stop completely when the leaves begin to wither. Dry, warm winter for the tubers until forcing begins in February.

Light: No direct sunshine, best in a semi-shaded location.

Heat: High indoor temperature in growth and flowering periods February–October (minimum 22° C. (75° F.)). Keep the tubers at minimum 15° C. (60° F.) through the winter.

Air: Humid air. Avoid drops of water on leaves and flowers. Avoid draughts.

Re-potting: Put the tubers in flat pots or dishes in February–March and cover them with 2 cm. (1 in.) of soil.

Propagation: By seeding, leaf cuttings or stem cuttings.

Pests: Greenfly.

Diseases: Brown, rolled-up edges caused by air which is too dry.

Varieties: 'Gierts Rote' (red), 'Gierts Weisse' (white), 'Kaiser Friedrich' (scarlet with white edges) and 'Kaiser Wilhelm' (blue with white edges).

Smithiantha hybrida

NOTE: The tubers, which are sold in same way as those of the Tubero begonia, may be forced in the identi manner by placing in peat in a wa flower window in February, followed potting.

Smithiantha hybrida

Habitat: Mexico.

Growth: Tuberous plant, with upri, stems, densely covered with down. heart-shaped, green, downy leaves h dark brown patterns along their ve The bell-shaped, two-lipped, hang flowers are borne in petiolate cluste the upper side is scarlet, the unders yellow and the throat yellow with cr son spots. Flowering period, Ju October.

Use: Ornamental, both as a foliage pl and a flower plant. The leaves and ste are brittle, and must be handled v care during transport and daily att tion.

Soil: Soilless mixture or leaf mo with peat and sand mixed in. G drainage.

Feeding: 3 grams per litre (1 oz. gallon) of water every 2 weeks, beg

ing 1 month after the start of growth, nd ending when flowering begins.
Vater: Large amounts of water at room ~mperature in spring and summer, until owering ceases. After that, reduce the mounts gradually until the parts of the ~ant which are above the surface of ~e soil wither away. Keep the tubers ~y during the winter.
ight: Semi-shaded spot.
~eat: From the time the tuber is planted March until flowering begins in June, ~inimum 25° C. (77° F.). During and ~ter flowering, June–October, minimum 20° C. (70° F.). Keep the tuber dry ~ring winter from November to ~bruary at minimum 12° C. (55° F.).
~ir: Dry air, but will not stand spraying drops of water on leaves and flowers.
~e-potting: Place the tubers, several ~gether, into a flat dish, and cover with ~m. (1 in.) of soil in February.
~opagation: By division of tubers in ~bruary.
~sts: Red spider mites and thrips in air ~ich is too dry.
~seases: Round, brown spots on leaves ~e caused by watering with water ~ich is too cold.

~reptocarpus hybridus (124)

~abitat: South Africa.
~owth: Herbaceous biennial with ~arse, wrinkled leaves; these are vir- ~ally stemless, and collected in a strong ~sette. There are 2–3 trumpet-shaped ~wers on each stem in white, pink, ~e, violet or red, many with veins in ~er colours and spots on the throat. ~ten flowers the whole year round.
~e: Good indoor plant, which is easier cultivate than most other of the ~sneriaceae. Attractive flowering in plant's second year of life.
~il: Nourishing loam, with the addition ~peat and sand, possibly soilless mix- ~e.
~ding: 3 grams per litre (1 oz. per ~lon) of water every week (April–

September). Only give nourishment to damp soil balls.
Water: Plenty in summer, but do not allow to dry out; moderate in winter.
Light: Semi-shaded spot, lighter in winter.
Heat: Normal room temperature, but not less than minimum 15° C. (60° F.).
Air: Preferably damp air in the summer.
Re-potting: February. Take care not to break the very brittle stems.
Propagation: By seed or leaf cuttings.
Pests: Red spider mites (in too much sunshine), greenfly and thrips.
NOTE: One of the best indoor plants for flower windows in semi-shaded locations.

Acanthaceae

Aphelandra squarrosa (125)

Zebra Plant, Tiger Plant

Habitat: Brazil.
Growth: Tough stem. Large, shiny, pointed, oval leaves, arranged in cross formation, with silvery-white or yellowish markings along the veins. The yellow flowers are collected in a pyramidal inflorescence, each one supported by stiff, yellow bracts. Flowers for 6 weeks between April and August.
Use: Hothouse plant, suitable for conservatories or warm flower windows.
Soil: Heavy, nourishing loam.
Feeding: 3 grams per litre (1 oz. per gallon) of water every week (March–August).
Water: Plenty in summer; winter, moderate.
Light: Semi-shaded location.
Heat: Thrives best at minimum 22° C. (70° F.) the whole year round. At temperatures below 18° C. (65° F.) no flowers will appear. At temperatures above 24° C. (75° F.) the leaves will distort and become unattractive.
Air: High degree of air humidity, otherwise the leaves will roll up.

Re-potting: March.
Cutting: Cut back after flowering has ceased. Otherwise, the plant will tend to become long and spindly.
Propagation: By cuttings in May over a minimum 30° C. (85° F.) bottom heat.
Pests: Scale insects, greenfly.
Diseases: Brown marks on leaves and rolled-up edges are due to air which is too dry, distorted leaves to air temperatures which are too high (over minimum 24° C. (75° F.)).
Varieties: 'Dania' is typical of a few, new, compact varieties with several flower stems. Will stand winter at slightly lower temperatures (minimum 12–15° C. (55–60° F.)), without reduction in the level of flowering.

Beloperone guttata (126)

Shrimp Plant

Habitat: Mexico.
Growth: Evergreen bush with green branches and smooth, pointed, oval leaves. The flowers are white with a purple-red spot on the lower lip, hanging and surrounded by reddish-brown, overlapping bracts in a large, pendulous inflorescence. The individual flowers are not very long-lasting, but the bracts preserve the decorative effect for months on end. Flowers the whole year round. No real resting period.
Use: The only member of the *Acanthaceae* which is suitable for indoor culture. The others are best cultivated in conservatories or greenhouses.
Soil: Porous, strong loam with sand and peat added.
Feeding: 3 grams per litre (1 oz. per gallon) of water every week (February–September). Only give nourishment to damp soil balls.
Water: Moderate the whole year round, without allowing to dry out.
Light: As light as possible, away from direct sunlight. If too strongly shaded, the top leaves will lose their reddish-brown colour.

Crossandra infundibuliformis

Heat: Normal room temperature. W[...] ter, minimum 18° C. (65° F.). If the te[...] perature is too high, the shoots beco[...] long and spindly.
Air: Slightly damp air.
Re-potting: February.
Cutting: Occasionally prune top sho[...] in order to achieve a more comp[...] growth.
Propagation: By top cuttings in April[...]
Pests: Greenfly.
Diseases: Leaves roll up or fall if [...] soil ball becomes too dry.
Varieties: 'Nørgards Favorite' w[...] compact growth and dense bracts.

Crossandra infundibuliformis

Habitat: India.
Growth: Low sub-shrub with sligh[...] undulating, shiny, dark green lea[...] Upright flower spike with collar[...] orange flowers. Vigorous and lo[...] flowering, often the whole year round[...]
Use: Hothouse plant.
Soil: Garden loam, with leaf mo[...] peat and sand added.
Feeding: 2 grams per litre ($\frac{1}{2}$ oz. [...] gallon) of water every week (Februa[...] September), but never to dry soil ball[...]
Water: Plenty in summer; win[...] moderate, but do not allow to dry [...] Use water at minimum 25° C. (77° F[...]
Light: Semi-shaded location.

Heat: Summer, minimum 22° C. 72° F.); winter, never below minimum 5° C. (60° F.).
Air: Absolutely damp air. In dry air the leaves will roll up.
Re-potting: February, in flat pots.
Propagation: By cuttings in spring, possibly by seeding.
Pests: Red spider mites.
Diseases: Leaves roll up as a result of dry air or too much light; watering with water which is too cold causes brown spots on leaves.
Varieties: 'Mona Wallhed' with larger, darker and longer-lasting flowers.
NOTE: Unusual flower colour for a pot plant.

Fittonia verschaffeltii (127)

Habitat: Peru.
Growth: Creeping plant, only 10 cm. (4 in.) high, with oval leaves which have coloured veins. The flower spikes are without ornamental value.
Use: Hothouse plant for ground cover ing in a warm, damp conservatory or flower window.
Soil: Light, humus-rich soil, leaf mould and sand.
Feeding: 2 grams per litre ($\frac{1}{2}$ oz. per gallon) of water every 2 weeks (March–August).
Water: Keep the soil damp without watering too much.
Light: Shaded or semi-shaded location.
Heat: Minimum 22–25° C. (72–77° F.) the whole year round.
Air: Absolutely damp air. Spray with rain water, which will not produce spots the leaves.
Re-potting: Spring, in flat pots.
Cutting: Stopping the shoots gives a bushier plant. The flower shoots can be removed when they appear.
Propagation: By cuttings in the spring.
Pests: Slugs and snails, wood lice, greenfly.
Other species: argyroneura (illustrated) with silvery-white leaf veins; *pearcei*

with crimson leaf veins. Planting the two together will give an attractive combination which will provide a 'forest floor' in a warm conservatory.

Jacobinia carnea

Habitat: Brazil.
Growth: Vigorous, square, branched stems. Oval, downy, grey-green leaves. Dense inflorescences with 5 cm. (2 in.) long, rose-red flowers which open simultaneously.
Use: Hothouse plant, flowering in the summer. Best in conservatories.
Soil: Garden loam, rich in humus, or possibly soilless mixture.
Feeding: 2 grams per litre ($\frac{1}{2}$ oz. per gallon) of water every week (March–August).
Water: Plenty the whole year round. The soil balls must never be allowed to dry out.
Light: Semi-shaded location.
Heat: Constant, minimum 20–22° C. (68–74° F.).
Air: Damp air the whole year round.
Re-potting: February, after thorough watering.
Cutting: Stop young plants, so as to obtain more bushy growth. Cut away withered inflorescences.

Jacobinia carnea

Ruellia devosiana

Propagation: By cuttings in spring.
Pests: Greenfly, red spider mites.
Diseases: Rolled up leaf edges are caused by air which is too dry.
Other species: See below.

Jacobinia pohliana

Growth: More vigorous and robust than *Jacobinia carnea*. The leaves are bigger and softer, the inflorescences longer. Use and culture otherwise the same.

Jacobinia paucifolia

Growth: Well-branched stems, growing about 30 cm. (12 in.) high. The nodding tube-like flowers, which are scarlet with yellow tips, are positioned individually on short stems in the axils. Flowers, unlike the other *Jacobinia* types, in late winter (February–April).
Use: Ornamental indoor plant when in flower, winter and early spring.
Culture: As for *Jacobinia carnea*, but does not require quite so much warmth. May sometimes be left out of doors to spend the summer in a warm spot. Bring inside before the first night frost, and place in a cool spot (minimum 10°C. (50°F.)) from October to December. After that, at minimum 18°C. (65°F.) during the flowering period. Re-pot after flowering has ceased in May.

246

Ruellia devosiana

Habitat: Brazil.
Growth: 30 cm. (12 in.) high, wel branched half-bush. The leaves are ov and pointed with velvety, dark gree upper sides having white patterns alon the veins, and red undersides. Funne shaped, pale mauve flowers, winter an spring.
Use: Best in a shaded flower windo with damp air. Worth while both as foliage plant and a flower plant. Mo attractive as an annual.
Soil: Porous soil, rich in humus, wi leaf mould, clay and sand added. Goo drainage.
Feeding: 1 gram per litre ($\frac{1}{4}$ oz. per ga lon) of water every 2 weeks (March August). The roots become scorched there is too high a concentration of sa in the soil.
Water: Constantly damp soil. Use wat at minimum 25°C. (77°F.).
Light: Semi-shaded location. Will n stand direct sunshine.
Heat: Summer, normal temperatur winter, not below minimum 15° (60°F.).
Air: Damp air. Grows badly in centr heating. Avoid draughts.
Re-potting: After flowering has ceas in spring, in flat pots.
Cutting: Prune young plants in the su mer, to produce compact growth. Ol plants are inclined to go bare lower dov They should then be discarded and placed by young plants from cuttings.
Propagation: By cuttings in June o 25°C. (77°F.) bottom heat.
Pests: Red spider mites, thrips.
Diseases: Rolled-up leaves are the res of too dry air and too much sun.

Thunbergia alata (12

Black-eyed Susan

Habitat: South-eastern Africa.
Growth: Perennial, herbaceous, twini plant with decorative, spear-sha

eaves and large, flat-collared, orange-yellow flowers with blackish-violet throats. Summer-flowering.
Use: May be cultivated as a perennial, but as a rule is treated as an annual, with seeding in the spring. Requires plenty of space in a large-light window with a cord or net trellis. Very rapid growth. Can also be used in a warm spot out of doors.
Soil: Soilless mixture.
Feeding: 3 grams per litre (1 oz. per gallon) of water every week, throughout the growth period.
Water: Plenty; must not dry out completely.
Light: Location as light and airy as possible; full sunlight will do very well.
Heat: Normal summer temperature.
Air: Spraying in hot weather.
Propagation: Seeding in sand and peat in February. The seedlings should be kept evenly moist in a light spot at minimum 15° C. (60° F.).
Re-potting: Transplant to permanent pots when the plants are about 10 cm. (4 in.) high.
Tying up: The trellis must be ready before the plant is taken to its permanent spot. Tie up at the start to avoid the plant tangling.
Cutting: When growth is particularly vigorous, some of the trails must be cut away, in order to assist flowering.
Pests: Red spider mites.
Other species: See below.

Thunbergia grandiflora

Habitat: India.
Growth: Vigorous twining bush with large, slightly bell-shaped, light blue flowers.
Use: Cultivated in large pots or tubs which are planted out in warm conservatories.
Culture: As for *Thunbergia alata*, but not as an annual. Requires more warmth, even during the winter season. Cut back after flowering has ceased in

November. Re-pot after growth begins in early spring.

Labiatae

Coleus blumei   (129)

Coleus

Habitat: Tropical Africa and Asia.
Growth: Square succulent stems. Oval, pointed, saw-toothed leaves with a variety of patterns in many colours. Light-blue flowers in light inflorescences.
Use: Foliage plant, most attractive in its first year.
Soil: Soilless mixture or pure peat with rotten leaves added. pH 4 (very acid soil).
Feeding: 3 grams per litre ($\frac{3}{4}$ oz. per gallon) of water every 2 weeks (March–September).
Water: Moderate the whole year round, less in the resting period, September–January. For preference, use rainwater.
Light: The full colour of the leaves only emerges with strong light, preferably full sunlight, and disappears during the winter.
Heat: Normal room temperature; winter, not below minimum 15° C. (60° F.).
Air: Spray in hot weather.
Re-potting: February, and possibly again in June.
Cutting: Cut back on re-potting in spring, which will counteract the tendency for the lower parts of the stem to become bare.
Propagation: By cuttings or by seeding in February–March.
Pests: Greenfly.
Varieties: Large numbers of varieties with many different leaf colours: 'Bienvenu' (red, with narrow yellow edges), 'Fanal' (dark red), 'Candidum' (whitish-red), 'Pink Rainbow' (salmon pink) and 'Red Rainbow' (red).
NOTE: Best results are obtained in a sunny location; water with rainwater and strong fertiliser.
Other species: See below.

Coleus pumilus

Habitat: Philippines.
Growth: Creeping or hanging stems. The leaves are brown with green edges. There are hybrids and varieties with crimson leaves which have patterns in brown, gold and green. Numerous inflorescences with sky-blue flowers in winter.
Use: Good hanging-bowl plant.
Culture: As for *Coleus blumei*, but require higher temperature and more water in the winter season.

Glechoma hederacea

Ground Ivy

Habitat: Europe (Great Britain).
Growth: Creeping, metre-long (3-ft.) almost wire-like stems. Small, kidney-shaped, round-indented leaves. Upright flower shoots in the axils, and the violet lip-flowers have spots on their throats. Anthers form two crosses. Flowering period, May–June.
Use: Undemanding hanging-bowl plant. May sometimes be left to spend the summer out of doors, e.g. in a balcony-box.
Soil: Leaf mould mixed with sand.

Glechoma hederacea fol. var.

Feeding: 2 grams per litre ($\frac{1}{2}$ oz. per gallon) of water every 2 weeks (April–August).
Water: Summer, normal watering; winter, relatively dry.
Light: Shaded or semi-shaded location.
Heat: Cool room. Winter, minimum 5°C. (40°F.).
Air: Slightly humid air. Spray in hot weather.
Re-potting: Spring, as required.
Propagation: By division.
Variant: foliis variegatis, with white variegated leaves. Greater ornamental value than the main type.

Plectranthus fruticosus

Habitat: South Africa.
Growth: Evergreen sub-shrub, up to a metre (over 3 ft.) high. The leaves are oval, saw-tooth edged and bristly, with reddish stems. When rubbed they give off an aromatic fragrance which was at one time thought to drive away moth. Pale blue flowers in upright clusters in late winter and spring.
Use: Easily satisfied, vigorous plant for indoor locations.
Soil: Garden soil rich in humus.
Feeding: 3 grams per litre (1 oz. per gallon) of water every 2 weeks (April–August).
Water: Moderate the whole year round, least during the resting period, August–January.
Light: Will stand full sunlight.
Heat: Quite indifferent to warmth. In winter, minimum 8°C. (47°F.) is enough, but the plant will stand normal room temperature.
Air: Will stand any indoor air.
Re-potting: Late spring after flowering has ceased.
Cutting: Will take vigorous pruning in the interests of better formation.
Propagation: By cuttings which are taken after flowering.
Pests: Greenfly on young shoots.
Other species: See below.

Plectranthus australis (130)

Habitat: Australia.

Growth: Creeping or hanging stems which are a reddish-brown colour. The leaves are a monotone green on both upper and undersides.

Use: Easily satisfied hanging-bowl plant.

Culture: As for *Plectranthus fruticosus.* Will not stand drying out altogether.

Plectranthus oertendahlii

Growth: Creeping or hanging stems. Dark green leaves with silvery-white stripes along the veins like a net over the surface of the leaf. Pure white flowers in dense, upright clusters in September–October.

Use: Easily satisfied hanging-bowl plant.

Culture: As for *Plectranthus fruticosus.*

Verbenaceae

Clerodendrum thomsoniae

Habitat: Tropical West Africa.

Growth: Summer green, climbing bush, up to 4 m. (13 ft.) high. The leaves are opposite, pointed, oval, and plain edged. Large flower clusters from March to July. The individual flower consists of a heart-shaped, white calyx, which encloses the blood-red flower, hence the popular name 'Bleeding Heart'. The plant loses its leaves in the resting period, October–February.

Use: Twining indoor plant which needs a strong trellis and a lot of space.

Soil: Light soil, rich in humus.

Feeding: 3 grams per litre (1 oz. per gallon) of water every 2 weeks (March–August).

Water: Summer, normal watering. From September reduce the amounts gradually and leave the plant dry in the winter, as for *Fuchsia.* From February,

more water again and a higher temperature.

Light: Light growth location away from direct sunlight.

Heat: Normal room temperature during growth period. In winter, minimum 5° C. (40° F.). From February, minimum 10° C. (50° F.), rising to normal room temperature.

Air: Frequent spraying, especially in the spring.

Cutting: Prune vigorously on re-potting. The flowers only develop on the year's new shoots. Can be developed as a standard with a trunk by pruning.

Propagation: By cuttings in the spring.

Pests: Red spider mites.

NOTE: Flowering is only satisfactory when the resting period (October–February) is adhered to, and pruning is undertaken subsequently. During the resting time temperature should be minimum 5° C. (40° F.), there should be plenty of light and the plant kept almost dry.

Other species: See below.

Clerodendrum speciosissimum (131)

Growth: Shrub, not a climbing plant. Bright scarlet flowers in large, loose inflorescences in June–September. Black berries

Use and culture: As for *Clerodendrum thomsoniae,* but does not have quite such a marked resting period. In the first year stopping is omitted, and the plant will then flower at the tip of the main stem.

Clerodendrum fragrans

Growth: Bush form, with white or very pale red flowers which have a soporific fragrance. Flowers the whole year round, with short pauses.

Use and culture: As for *Clerodendrum thomsoniae,* but the winter resting period is unnecessary.

Lantana camara (132)

Habitat: Tropical America.
Growth: Small, deciduous bush, with grey-green, oval leaves. The flowers lie in dense, circular inflorescences, with the oldest and darkest flowers on the outside, progressively lighter flowers towards the centre and the buds lightest of all. The old flowers wither and fall, and are replaced by the newly opened buds. The duration of the individual inflorescences may range over several months. Often black, berry-like fruits. Varieties are to be found with white, yellow, pink, red and bicoloured (scarlet/orange) flowers.
Use: Long-flowering indoor plant for sunny room. Also, quite suitable for a balcony-box and plant-tub out of doors. Standard plants can be grown.
Soil: Soilless mixture.
Feeding: 3 grams per litre (1 oz. per gallon) of water every week (April–September). Only give nourishment to damp soil balls.
Water: Light, dry soil is to be preferred; hence water sparingly. Never water through a base dish, and make sure there is good drainage from balcony-boxes or plant-tubs.
Light: As much light and sunshine as possible.
Heat: Summer, normal temperature; winter, minimum 10° C. (50° F.).
Air: Dry air, especially during the winter.
Re-potting: February.
Cutting: Older plants may be shaped by stopping the main growths in February. A standard may be formed by allowing a single shoot to run up in the air, supported by a bamboo cane. All side shoots should be removed, and the crown develops where the top shoot is nipped.
Propagation: By cutting in September and/or February.
Pests: Red spider mites.
NOTE: Excellent sunshine plant.

250

Oleaceae

Jasminum odoratissimum

Habitat: Canary Islands and Madeira.
Growth: Long, slender, green shoots with 3-segmented leaves. The yellow flowers are produced in small inflorescences, and are delicately fragrant. Flowering is not abundant, but distributed over the whole of the year.
Use: Pot plant or climbing plant, which requires some support.
Soil: Soilless mixture.
Feeding: 2 grams per litre ($\frac{1}{2}$ oz. per gallon) of water every week (March–September).
Water: Even watering the whole year round, but more sparing during the winter.
Light: As much as possible, but no scorching sunshine.
Heat: Normal room temperature.
Air: Spray during the spring.
Re-potting: February.
Cutting: Inclined to shed its bottom leaves. This can be counteracted to some extent by shortening the growths which will also distribute the flowers more evenly.
Propagation: By cuttings.
Other species: See below.

Jasminum odoratissimum

Jasminum officinale grandiflorum

Habitat: The Orient.
Growth: Small, 5–7-lobed leaves. Pleasant smelling, white flowers in cymes in the shoot tips from June to September.
Use and culture: As for *Jasminum odoratissimum.*

Jasminum polyanthum (133)

Jasmine

Habitat: China.
Growth: Small-lobed leaves on reddish branches. White, powerfully fragrant flowers in the spring. Can be forced into flower up to Christmas.
Use and culture: As for *Jasminum odoratissimum.*

Jasminum mesnyi

Habitat: China.
Growth: Square stems. Three-lobed evergreen leaves. Large yellow flowers in the axils on summer shoots, but no fragrance.
Use and culture: As for *Jasminum odoratissimum.*

Jasminum sambac

Habitat: Eastern Asia, where the flowers are used in temples as offerings to Buddha.
Growth: Upright growth. Oval, pointed leaves. Semi-double, white flowers with a delightful fragrance from early spring till late autumn.
Use and culture: As for *Jasminum odoratissimum,* but requires higher temerature (minimum 25° C. (77° F.)).

Loganiaceae

Nicodemia diversifolia

Habitat: Madagascar.
Growth: Evergreen bush with branches, cinnamon-brown stems and

Nicodemia diversifolia

indented, succulent green leaves, which are reminiscent of oak leaves. No flowering of any significance.
Use: Foliage plant for cool, shady locations, e.g. windows facing north.
Soil: Loam with peat added.
Feeding: 3 grams per litre (1 oz. per gallon) of water every week (April–August).
Water: Summer, plenty; winter, sparingly.
Light: Shade.
Heat: Cool location. Summer, minimum 15° C. (60° F.), winter, minimum 8° C. (47° F.).
Air: Normal indoor air. Spray in hot weather in the summer season.
Re-potting: February.
Cutting: Nip young plants in order to obtain better umbrella-like branching.
Propagation. By cuttings, April–May.
Pests: Red spider mites.

Apocynaceae

Allamanda neriifolia (134)

Habitat: Brazil.
Growth: Tall, slightly twining bush, with evergreen, oleander-like leaves. Large, funnel-shaped, yellow flowers with dark stripes in the funnels. Delicate fragrance.
Use: Best in a light conservatory or large flower window facing south.
Soil: Loam, rich in humus, with the addition of peat, leaf mould and gravel.

Feeding: 5 grams per litre (1½ oz. per gallon) of water every week (April–August).

Water: Plenty of water in summer; winter, moderate.

Light: Light and sunny location.

Heat: Summer, normal room temperature. Winter, not below minimum 15° C. (60° F.).

Air: Damp air with frequent spraying in spring and summer.

Re-potting: February.

Cutting: Cut back old shoots in February.

Propagation: By cuttings over high bottom heat in February.

Pests: Red spider mites.

Other species: See below.

Allamanda cathartica

Growth: Vigorous, twining shrub. Funnel-shaped, yellow flowers with a delicate fragrance.

Use and culture: As for *Allamanda neriifolia.*

Variant: 'Hendersonii', with large bell-shaped, warm-yellow flowers having a delicate fragrance. Reddish buds.

Dipladenia boliviensis

Habitat: Bolivia.

Growth: 2-m. (6-ft.)-high twining plant with smooth, oval leaves. Trumpet-shaped, white flowers with yellow throats, hanging in clusters from the end of the 1-year shoot. Flowering period, May–November.

Use: Long-flowering twining plant for windows facing east or west in not too intense heat.

Soil: Loam, rich in nourishment, with good drainage.

Feeding: 2 grams per litre (½ oz. per gallon) of water every week (April–August). Only give nourishment to damp soil balls.

Water: Summer, normal; winter, moder-

ate. Avoid lingering moisture or wate in the base dish.

Light: Light location away from direc sunshine.

Heat: Summer, 16–18° C. (60–65° F.) winter, minimum 14–16° C. (55–60° F.), but not cooler.

Air: Dry indoor air with spraying i summer.

Re-potting: February, in pots which ar not too large. Wet thoroughly before re potting.

Cutting: Cutting back in February wi assist the formation of young sid shoots which are likely to flower.

Propagation: By cuttings with botto heat.

Pests: Red spider mites.

Diseases: Curled leaves are the result too dry air or too intense sunlight.

Other species: See below.

Dipladenia amoena rubiniana

Growth: Vigorous plant with larg scabrous, furrowed, shaggy, almo black-green leaves. The flowers are deep pink colour.

Use and culture: As for *Dipladenia bo viensis.*

Dipladenia sanderi   (13

Growth: Shiny, fresh-green leave Large, pink flowers with yellow throat

Use and culture: As for *Dipladenia bo viensis.*

NOTE: This type is often sold in the for of small plants in flower under the nar 'Sanderi rosea'. A short time afterwar they will produce twining runners whi must be tied to net or bamboo trellises

Nerium oleander   (13

Oleander

Habitat: Mediterranean countries.

Growth: Vigorous, evergreen bush wi soft branches and lance-shaped, cor ceous, grey-green leaves. There are al orms with variegated leaves. The inflorescences grow at the tips of the 1-year shoots. White, pink or red flowers from July until September. Delicate fragrance. *All parts of the plant are highly poisonous.*

Use: Young plants are very suitable for window-sills or flower windows; older plants should be used as tub-plants for conservatories. May sometimes be left out doors for the summer in a warm spot.

Soil: Strong loam with the addition of peat, gravel and a basic fertiliser in the form of bonemeal.

Feeding: 5 grams per litre (1½ oz. per gallon) of water every week (April–August).

Water: Grows—in the wild state—in river beds which have dried up in the summer, with its roots striking into the damp soil. So, give plenty of water from early spring right through until October. The pot or tub should stand in a spacious base dish, which is filled a few times each week with water at minimum 30°C. (86°F.). It is quite all right to have water in the dish for long periods. Give more moderate amounts in the winter, but always with the chill taken off.

Light: Likes a lot of light and full sun shine.

Heat: Normal temperature in summer; winter resting period at minimum 5°C. (40°F.).

Air: Dry air. No spraying. When left to spend the summer out of doors the plant should not be exposed to long periods of rain.

Re-potting: February, in spacious pots or tubs. The roots require a lot of space.

Cutting: Prune young shoots. Trunk-trees with 150-cm. (almost 5-ft.) trunks may be trimmed slightly by the removal of all side shoots and suckers.

Propagation: By cuttings in May. May strike roots in water.

Pests: Scale insects, mealy-bugs.

NOTE: The entire plant contains the deadly poisons, nerein and oleandrin.

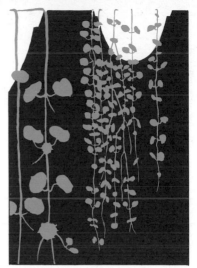

Ceropegia linearis woodii

Asclepiadaceae

Ceropegia linearis woodii

Habitat: Natal.

Growth: Hanging plant with wire-thin runners about a metre (over 3 ft.) long. Heart shaped, silvery grey, marbled leaves on short stems. In every axil there are 2–3 flesh-coloured, lantern-shaped flowers. Thickened aerial tubers on the runners. Flowering all year round.

Use: 'Different' hanging plant for windows facing south.

Soil: Very porous soil, e.g. soilless mixture, with sand added.

Feeding: 2 grams per litre (¼ oz. per gallon) of water every 2 weeks (April–July)

Water: Moderate in summer without lingering moisture. Winter, almost completely dry.

Light: Very light location (sun from the south).

Heat: Summer, normal temperature; winter, minimum 8°C. (47°F.). Will not stand high winter temperatures.

Air: Dry air.
Re-potting: February, in small pots.
Propagation: By shoot cuttings, or off-shoots from aerial tubers which will take root.

Hoya bella (137)

Habitat: Java.
Growth: Hanging plant with light, pointed leaves and hanging flower clusters; the long-lasting flowers are pale pink with purple in the centre. Many flowering periods from April to October, with a few weeks' pause in between each.
Use: As a hanging-bowl plant, since the hanging flower clusters must be seen from below for the best effect.
Soil: Good garden soil, with clay, leaf mould and gravel added.
Feeding: 4 grams per litre ($1\frac{1}{4}$ oz. per gallon) of water every 3 weeks (February–July).
Water: Moderate. The roots will not stand too much watering or lingering moisture. From October to January, almost completely dry.
Light: Prefers a semi-shaded location.
Heat: Will stand a high summer temperature. Winter, minimum 15–20° C. (60–70° F.).
Air: Prefers damp air.
Re-potting: Young plants have to be re-potted every spring in February, older plants very seldom. The top layer of soil may need to be renewed (top-dressing).
Propagation: By cuttings in the spring.
Pests: Mealy bugs, scale insects.
Other species: See below.

Hoya carnosa (138)

Wax Flower

Habitat: Eastern Asia.
Growth: Evergreen twining plant with several long (1 m., or more than 3 ft.) greenish-brown shoots with aerial roots. Pointed, oval fleshy, smooth, dark green leaves. Inflorescences develop on small knotty, perennial stems, which must no[t] be removed since it is here that the nex[t] year's flowers are formed. The indivi[-] dual flower is star-shaped, its thic[k] waxy-white petals have a red centra[l] spot, and there are 12–15 flowers i[n] every spherical umbel. There is a deli[-] cate fragrance, and the blossoms secret[e] drops of nectar.
Use: Twining plant on firm trellises i[n] windows or against walls, indoors, i[n] conservatories or on verandas.
Culture: As for *Hoya bella*, but prefe[rs] dry air and more light. Best in a windo[w] facing east or west, possibly a light wi[n-] dow facing north, away from direct su[n-] shine. Winter temperature, minimu[m] 12–15° C. (55–60° F.). When the ne[w] leaf shoots develop, raise the tempera[-] ture to 20° C. (70° F.).
Cutting: Old flower stems must not b[e] removed. Long, apparently leafless tra[ils] are often formed, which must not be c[ut] away but tied up to the trellis, as the[y] later form leaves in the normal way.
Tying up: Trails are only tied on on[e] side of the trellis, as the plant has [a] distinct 'front' and 'back', and alwa[ys] turns the upper surface of the leaves [to] the one side.

Stapelia variegata

Habitat: South Africa.
Growth: Succulent, with finger-thic[k] upright shoots. The flower is shaped li[ke] a 5-cornered star, and is light bro[wn] with dark brown spots in attractive pa[t-] terns. When it emerges it has a disti[nct] carrion smell, which attracts flies to l[ay] eggs in it, therefore the fly larvae ta[ke] care of the flower's pollination.
Use: Very suitable for cactus windo[ws] in full sunshine from the south.
Soil: Cactus soil with clay, sand, p[eat] and crocks. Good drainage.
Feeding: 2 grams per litre ($\frac{1}{2}$ oz. [per] gallon) of water every 3 weeks (Marc[h–] July).

Stapelia variegata

Water: Spring and summer, moderate watering with drying-out in between. From September gradually reduce the quantities. In winter, almost completely dry.
Light: Sunshine.
Heat: Summer, normal room temperature; winter, minimum 8°C. (47°F.).
Air: Dry indoor air.
Re-potting: Seldom.
Propagation: By shoot cuttings in the spring.

Stephanotis floribunda (139)

Habitat: Madagascar.
Growth: Vigorous twining plant with several shoots about a metre (over 3 ft.) long. The dark green leaves are oval and coriaceous, and in the axils are 8–10 white, fragrant, tubular flowers with flat tubes. Flowering period, May–October.
Use: Twining plant for trellises and walls indoors, in conservatories and on verandas.
Soil: Soilless mixture.
Feeding: 3 grams per litre (1 oz. per gallon) of water every week (March–October).
Water: Needs a lot of water during the growth and flowering periods. Must never be allowed to dry out, but should never have standing water in the base dish. Winter, moderate watering, without extended periods of drought.
Light: Windows facing east or west.
Heat: Summer, normal temperature; winter, minimum 12–15°C. (55–60°F.).
Air: Dry air.
Re-potting: January, in pots which are not too small.
Tying up: Tie up young shoots regularly, so that the leaves and flowers can unfold freely. The plant has a tendency to flower in the tips of new shoots (right up at the top), therefore the trellising should be arranged so that the young shoots are distributed evenly over the whole of the plant.
Propagation: By cuttings over 25°C. (77°F.) minimum bottom heat, in the spring.
Pests: Scale insects, mealy bugs.
Diseases: Yellow spots on leaves are the result of too harsh sunlight; leaves turning completely lemon-yellow are the result of drought.

Rubiaceae

Bouvardia domestica

Habitat: Central America.
Growth: Evergreen bush with opposite leaves. The flowers are tubular, with 4-lobed collars, and are velvety on the outer sides. There are varieties in shades of white, pink and red. Flowering period, June–December.
Use: Flowering indoor plant for a light window or conservatory.
Soil: Strong loam with added peat, leaf mould and sand. pH 6·5.
Feeding: 2 grams per litre (½ oz. per gallon) of water every week (April–September).
Water: Summer, plenty; after flowering, sparingly.
Light: Window facing east or west.
Heat: Summer, warm (minimum 25°C. (77°F.)); autumn and winter, minimum 16°C. (60°F.). Flowers are long-lasting in relatively low temperature.
Air: Frequent spraying during the growth period.
Re-potting: Spring.

Cutting: Stopping main shoots in May will give better branching and a large number of flowers.
Propagation: By cuttings in April–May.
Pests: Greenfly, scale insects.
Diseases: Grey mould.
Other species: See below.

Bouvardia longifolia humboldtii (140)

Growth: A taller plant than the last species, with shining, rather leathery dark green leaves, and much larger fragrant white flowers which are up to 4 cm. ($1\frac{1}{2}$ in.) long and 2·5 cm. (1 in.) across, borne in less dense corymbs. Flowering period, September–December.
Use and culture: As for *Bouvardia domestica*, but will thrive under cooler conditions; summer, minimum 16°C. (60°F.); winter, minimum 13°C. (55°F.).

Coffea arabica (141)
Coffee

Habitat: Tropical Africa.
Growth: Branchy bush, with opposite, shiny, dark green leaves. Plants 3–4 years old have a profusion of star-shaped, fragrant white flowers from July to September. Cherry-like fruit, first green, then red and finally black, each one with two 'coffee beans'.
Use: Suitable for a large flower window in a semi-shaded location, in a conservatory or hall.
Soil: Soilless mixture with good drainage.
Feeding: 3 grams per litre (1 oz. per gallon) of water every 2 weeks (March–October).
Water: Plenty in summer, winter moderate. Will not stand lingering moisture.
Light: Semi-shaded location.
Heat: Normal room temperature with no major fluctuations, the whole year round. Soil temperature must never drop below 15°C. (60°F.).

Air: Damp air.
Re-potting: February–March, in spacious pots.
Cutting: Young plants have a single upright trunk with horizontal side branches, older plants are more branched. The plant can be adapted to the dimensions of the growth situation by nipping.
Propagation: By seeding completely fresh seeds over a minimum 25°C (77°F.) bottom heat in March, or by cuttings of top shoots (*not* side shoots).
Pests: Mealy bugs, scale insects. Wash the leaves down regularly.

Gardenia jasminoides (14?)
Gardenia

Habitat: Eastern Asia.
Growth: Evergreen bush with pointed, oval, full-edged, shiny leaves and white to yellowish-white double flowers with delicate fragrance. Flowering period May–October.
Use: Best in light window facing east or west.
Soil: Humus-rich loam, with peat and sand added. pH 3·5 (very acid soil).
Feeding: 4 grams per litre ($1\frac{1}{4}$ oz. per gallon) of water every 2 weeks (March–August). Only give nourishment to damp soil balls.
Water: Evenly damp soil the whole year round. Only use rainwater at minimum 20°C. (70°F.). If mains water containing calcium is to be used, add 1 gram ammonium sulphate per litre ($\frac{1}{4}$ oz. per gallon). The soil should never dry out but must also never remain damp and cold. Water must never be left in the base dish.
Light: Light window facing east or west.
Heat: The ideal mean temperature whole year round is minimum 16° (60°F.), as bud formation takes place at this temperature. Below a minimum 16°C. (60°F.), the buds do not form properly; above 18°C. (65°F.), the bud development is retarded in favour of leaf growth and the buds are shed. In

egetative period the temperature may
e allowed to rise to 25° C. (77° F.).

ir: Maintain constantly damp air,
specially in spring and early summer.
requent spraying at these times of the
ear, but not during the winter.

e-potting: February. Firm planting at
le same depth as previously.

ropagation: By cuttings over minimum
5° C. (77° F.) bottom heat in March or
eptember.

ests: Scale insects, mealy bugs.

iseases: Yellow leaves are the result of
atering with water which contains too
uch calcium and/or is too cold.

ariants: fortunei, with vigorous
owth, large leaves and large, double
wers; *plena,* the most commonly seen,
uble flowered; and *veitchii,* which also
as double flowers in the winter.

ora coccinea   (143)

ora

abitat: East Indies.

owth: Evergreen bush with shiny,
liptical leaves, and large, semi-
merical flower umbels having orange-
d or salmon-red flowers in the sum-
er.

e: Attractive, summer-flowering plant
light flower windows and conserva-
ies. Will not stand being moved dur-
g flowering. Newly purchased plants
en shed their flowers when they are
ced indoors. Repeated flowering after
climatisation.

il: Acid humus soil with peat and
d added. pH 4.

eding: 3 grams per litre (1 oz. per
lon) of water every week (March–
gust). Requires a great deal of nour-
ment in order to flower.

ter: Summer, normal watering
hout drying out and without linger-
water; winter, moderate. Use only
water warmed to room temperature;
me-containing mains water is used,
1 gram of ammonium sulphate per
e (¼ oz. per gallon).

Light: A lot of light, but away from
direct sunlight from the south.

Heat: High room temperature; winter,
not below minimum 18° C. (65° F.).
Soil temperature should also not be
allowed to fall below 18° C. (65° F.).

Air: Damp air with frequent spraying.

Re-potting: February. Older plants
should not be re-potted every year.

Cutting: Stop leading shoots frequently
during the growth period, as this will
assist the spreading of branches. When
the flower buds appear, cease nipping.

Propagation: By soft cuttings over minimum 25° C. (77° F.) bottom heat in
April.

Pests. Mealy bugs, scale insects.

Diseases: Rolled-up leaves are a sign of
too much sunlight; yellowing or falling
leaves are indicative of too low a soil
temperature or of watering with water
which is too cold.

Manettia inflata   (144)

Habitat: Tropical America.

Growth: Twining sub-shrub with oval,
fresh-green leaves. The tube-like scarlet
flowers have short, yellow crown lobes.
Flowers throughout the summer and
often throughout the year.

Use: Twining plant for light, not too
warm flower windows or conservatories.

Soil: Earth mould, rich in nourishment,
with peat and sand added.

Feeding: 2 grams per litre (½ oz. per
gallon) of water every week (February–
October).

Water: Summer, plenty; winter, moderate, but without drying out. Use rainwater or softened mains water.

Light: Plenty, but away from direct sun
light.

Heat: High indoor temperature. It is
important that the soil temperature
should not drop below minimum 18° C.
(65° F.).

Air: Damp air with frequent spraying,
spring and summer.

Re-potting: February. Older trellis

Lonicera japonica aureoreticulata

plants are difficult to re-pot. Instead, top dressing can be given, but taking care not to damage the roots.

Cutting: Cutting back after flowering has ceased will assist the new growth.

Tying up: Young plants must be tied up to a wire gauze or bamboo trellis.

Propagation: By cuttings over minimum 25° C. (77° F.) bottom heat.

Pests: Greenfly.

Diseases: Yellow leaves are due to cold and damp soil or to using water which is too cold.

Caprifoliaceae

Lonicera japonica aureoreticulata

Habitat: Japan.

Growth: Almost evergreen, twining plant with reddish stems and small, oval, pointed leaves, which are green with a network of yellow veins.

Use: Decorative trellis or hanging-bowl plant for rooms, conservatories and—under favourable conditions—out of doors (trellis facing south, with some sort of winter covering).

Soil: Loam with peat and sand added. pH 6.

Feeding: 2 grams per litre (½ oz. pe gallon) of water every week during th growth period.

Water: Summer, plenty; and no dryin out. Winter, almost dry.

Light: Window facing east, west north. In deep shade the vein patterns o the leaves are reduced.

Heat: Cool room temperature. Winte minimum 8° C. (45° F.).

Air: Fresh, airy spot.

Re-potting: Spring, before grow begins.

Cutting: Cut back, especially the th shoots, in February.

Tying up: Should be tied to bamb canes or trellis wire, before the tra become tangled with one another. C also be cultivated as a hanging plant.

Propagation: By cuttings in spring a summer.

Pests: Red spider mites, greenfly.

Viburnum tinus   (14

Laurustinus

Habitat: Mediterranean countries.

Growth: Evergreen bush with compa growth. Elliptical, shiny, dark gre leaves. White or pale pink, fragra flowers gathered into a rounded umb Normal flowering in May, but can forced from February to March.

Use: Tub plant in conservatories. C be left to spend the summer in a wa spot out of doors.

Soil: Strong, loam soil, rich in nouri ment, with sand and gravel added. Go drainage.

Feeding: 3 grams per litre (1 oz. gallon) of water every week (Marc September).

Water: Summer, plenty. Winter, j enough water to prevent the soil fr drying out. Leaves are shed, if co pletely dry.

Light: Light and airy spot; will sta full sunlight very well.

Heat: Summer, normal temperatu From November to January, minim

5° C. (40° F.), after that slow forcing at minimum 12° C. (55° F.).

Air: Dry air. Only spray during spring forcing.

Re potting: At intervals of 1 year, after flowering has ceased in May. At the same time the roots can be pruned to avoid having to use too big tubs.

Cutting: The plant is shaped by stopping young shoots.

Propagation: By cuttings in April or August.

Pests: Greenfly, mealy bugs, scale insects.

Campanulaceae

Campanula isophylla   (146–147)

Habitat: Italy.

Growth: Perennial with thin, hanging, very fragile stems, which exude a milky sap when lacerated. The short-stemmed grey-green leaves are down-covered. Large, open, star-shaped flowers.

Use: Well-known, easily satisfied indoor plant for window-sills or hanging-bowls. Can also be used as ground cover in conservatories, or—in the summer—out of doors in a balcony-box or flower-tub. Cultivated as an annual.

Soil: Strong, alkaline garden soil with gravel added.

Feeding: 2 grams per litre (¼ oz. per gallon) of water every week (April–July).

Water: Summer, plenty of water. From September, very dry. If kept for the winter, the plant should be kept light, dry and cool (minimum 5° C. (40° F.)).

Light: Very well-lit location. Full sunlight will do very well.

Heat: Cool room temperature. Winter, minimum 5° C. (40° F.). If kept warm during the winter, only a few flowers will be obtained.

Air: Normal indoor air.

Re-potting: February.

Propagation: By cuttings or division in the spring.

Diseases: Grey-mould and other fungus diseases are the result of soil or air which are too damp. Withering disease: Cause unknown, affected plants should be thrown out.

Variants: alba, with white flowers, and 'Mayii', with blue flowers and variegated leaves.

Compositae

Chrysanthemum morifolium hortorum   (148)

Chrysanthemum

Habitat: China.

Growth: Perennial with woody base and vigorous stems. The more or less indented leaves are dark green with pale undersides. The single daisy-shaped—or more or less double—flowers are to be found in all colours, except blue and violet.

Use: Vigorous varieties are used in gardens, cool houses or cool conservatories, planted out in the open or in pots; low, short-day treated types in pots as decoration indoors or on a balcony.

Soil: Heavy earth mould with gravel added. Good drainage.

Feeding: Plants in gardens and conservatories: 5 grams per litre (1½ oz. per gallon) every week from spring until flowering begins. Flowering indoor plants: no nourishment.

Water: Large consumption of water, especially in sunshine and warmth.

Light: Light and sunny spot.

Heat: Cool, especially during flowering. Should spend the winter at minimum 2° C. (36° F.). Short-day treated plants should be thrown out after flowering has ceased.

Air: Absolutely dry air.

Re-potting: Spring.

Cutting: Stopping the main shoot early in the year will produce bushy plants with a number of small flowers. If side shoots are rubbed off and the main heads restricted to one bud, there will be

Gerbera jamesonii

few flowers, but they will be large ones. This method is only to be used for the large-flowering varieties.

Propagation: By cuttings in the spring, or by division of older plants.

Pests: Greenfly.

Diseases: Mildew in too damp air.

NOTE: Short-day treated plants can be induced to flower at any time of the year by means of artificial 'short days' produced by keeping them in the dark or by giving extra light, as the case may be, in forcing houses. Such plants cannot be forced a second time, and should be thrown out after flowering has ceased indoors or in a conservatory.

Gazania splendens   (149)

Habitat: South Africa.

Growth: Low perennial with long, narrow leaves having white felt undersides and rolled-up edges. The flowers are large and marguerite-shaped, with yellow- or orange-edged crowns having a dark, eye-like pattern at the base; they only open in sunlight. Flowers the whole summer long.

Use: Flower plant for sunny windows facing south, conservatories or balcony-boxes or plant-tubs out of doors. Cultivated as a rule as an annual.

Soil: Soilless mixture.

Feeding: 2 grams per litre ($\frac{1}{2}$ oz. p⌐ gallon) of water every week (April⌐ September).

Water: Normal.

Light: Full sunlight.

Heat: High summer temperature. Ma⌐ possibly be allowed to winter at min⌐ mum 5° C. (40° F.).

Air: Dry air.

Re-potting: March–April.

Propagation: By cuttings in August, lik⌐ Pelargonia.

Gerbera jamesonii

Habitat: South Africa.

Growth: Perennial with deep roo⌐ Dandelion-like leaves, in rosettes a⌐ covered with down. The flowers grow ⌐ leafless stems; the ray florets are lo⌐ and pointed in white, yellow, red and ⌐ intermediate shades. The disk-flowe⌐ are yellow.

Use: Tub-plant for a conservatory. C⌐ be left to spend the summer in a war⌐ spot out of doors.

Soil: Sandy loam with peat adde⌐ pH 7·5. Use deep pots and tubs, sin⌐ the roots penetrate to a depth of 50 c⌐ (20 in.). Good drainage.

Feeding: 2 grams per litre ($\frac{1}{2}$ oz. ⌐ gallon) every week, April–August.

Water: Summer, plenty, without dryi⌐ out; winter, moderate.

Light: Sunny spot.

Ligularia tussilaginea

Heat: Summer, normal temperature. During the resting period in October–February, minimum 10°C. (50°F.), after which force at minimum 15°C. (60°F.).

Air: Normal dry air. During the growth period, however, spray frequently, but without wetting the flowers.

Re-potting: February, in deep pots or tubs.

Propagation: By seeding or division.

Pests: Greenfly, red spider mites.

Diseases: Fungus, which produces rot, is caused by cold, damp soil.

Ligularia tussilaginea

Habitat: Japan.

Growth: Herbaceous plant with long-stemmed, coltsfoot leaves, which are a glistening green colour with yellow spots and patterns. Yellow flowers have no ornamental value.

Use: Easily satisfied indoor or conservatory plant which will stand shade.

Soil: Soilless mixture in large, deep pots.

Feeding: 3 grams per litre (1 oz. per gallon) of water every week during the growth period.

Water: Summer, plenty; from October to February, very dry.

Light: Thrives in windows facing north.

Heat: Summer, normal room temperature; winter, minimum 15°C. (60°F.).

Air: Will stand dry indoor air.

Re-potting: February.

Propagation: By division in February.

Senecio cruentus (150)

Cineraria

Habitat: Canary Islands.

Growth: Herbaceous plant with large, heart-shaped, downy, dark green leaves. The composite flowers are collected into large inflorescences, which almost cover the foliage. All colours are represented. Flowering period from February to June, but the individual plants flower only for about 6 weeks indoors.

Senecio mikanioides

Use: Biennial indoor plant, which is thrown out after flowering has ceased.

Soil: Soilless mixture, best in plastic pots with low evaporation.

Feeding: No need to give nourishment during the short period the plant will be indoors.

Water: Large amounts, on hot days often twice a day; may be watered in a base dish. Must never be allowed to dry out.

Light: Light window. Best facing east or west. Strong sunlight will cause the colours to fade and will shorten the flowering period.

Heat: Cool (minimum 10–15°C. (50–60°F.).

Air: Spray in hot weather.

Re-potting: Throw the plant out after it has ceased flowering.

Propagation: By seed.

Pests: Greenfly, especially in draughts and sunlight. Spray the plant thoroughly or throw out when seriously affected by pest attack. The plant is often colloquially called 'bug plant'. Leaf miner.

Other species: See below.

Senecio mikanioides

German Ivy

Habitat: South Africa.

Growth: Climbing or hanging plant, with thin, ivy like, light green leaves. Very rapid growth. Flowers have no ornamental value.

Use: Hanging plant for cool rooms, e.g. conservatories, verandas or staircases.

Soil: Soilless mixture.

Feeding: 2 grams per litre ($\frac{1}{2}$ oz. per

gallon) of water every week (March–October).

Water: Summer, plenty; winter, moderate.

Light: Window facing north, or other shaded place.

Heat: Cool indoor air; winter, at the most 15° C. (60° F.).

Air: Dry air.

Re-potting: February.

Cutting: Cut back in February.

Propagation: By cuttings. The plant rapidly goes bare at its base, which is why frequent replacement by new plants is recommended.

Pests: Greenfly.

INDEX

Numbers of colour illustrations are indicated by italic figures.